Write Your Way Home

Write Your Way Home

Journaling for the brave

A wellbeing-through-writing guidebook

Dr Stephanie Dale

IWWI BOOKS

First published in Australia in 2024
by the International Wellbeing-through-writing Institute
ABN 60 889 920 117
www.iwwi.com.au

Copyright © Stephanie Dale 2024

This work is copyright. Apart from any use as permitted under the Copyright Act 1968, no part may be reproduced, copied, scanned, stored in a retrieval system, recorded, or transmitted, in any form or by any means, without the prior written permission of the publisher.

National Library of Australia
Dale, Stephanie, 1959–
Write Your Way Home: Journaling for the brave / Dr Stephanie Dale.
ISBN 978-0-9807043-3-4 (paperback)

 A catalogue record for this book is available from the National Library of Australia

Cover image by Duncan1890, iStock photo ID 72211930
Cover design by Stephanie Dale
Voyager Moon image design Stephanie Dale
Tree of life image by Migfoto, iStock photo ID 12652780
Triskelion image from Canva
Typesetting and eBook formatting by Sunset Publishing Services Pty Ltd

Acknowledgements
Robert Bly, 1989, *The Power of Shame*, in conversation with Michael Toms, New Digital Media.
Stephen Jenkinson, 2015, *Die Wise*, North Atlantic Books.
Kavisha Mazzella, 1998, "Wolf", from *Fisherman's Daughter*. Lyrics reprinted with kind permission of songwriter.
Barbara Mor and Monica Sjöö, 1987, *The Great Cosmic Mother*, HarperCollins.

This book is dedicated to every single brave heart
I met along *The Write Road*, and that is all of you.
Thank you, for what you have taught me about courage,
and the power of acting on the longing of the human spirit.
You are not the only ones whose life has been changed by this work.

To Ellen Day,
whom I met out there in the red dust country and
insisted I create a wellbeing writing program.
And so it began.
Thank you, Ellen, for your heart and your home.

To Marie Kelly,
who has championed the work in remote communities and
stepped forth bravely on her own writing journey.
Thank you Marie, for your ongoing support
and companionship in the demanding
heart of a dry desert.

Brunette. Respect, always.

Wolf out in the rain
Come by this gypsy fire
You're not the only one who's in pain
Sit here by the survivors.

Kavisha Mazzella

Contents

Welcome to Our Campfire vii
Chapter 1: The Write Road 1
Chapter 2: The Potent Forces 7
Chapter 3: Writing is a Waste of Time 11
Chapter 4: Writing is Good Medicine 15
Chapter 5: The Power Story 19
Chapter 6: The Only Question 22
Chapter 7: The Writer's Breath 27
Chapter 8: The Turning Times 31
Chapter 9: Try On the Orange 36

WRITING THE WHEEL: 12 writing journeys for life 41
   The Wheel of Life 43
   12-1: Embodied Journaling 46
   12-2: Every Body's Story 64
   12-3: The Story of Your Heart 79
   12-4: The Haunting 84
   12-5: The Book of the Dark 99
   12-6: Motherline 107
   12-7: The Crimes of Others 124
   12-8: Writing the Bones 155
   12-9: Writing the Wild 164
   12-10: Restoration 176
   12-11: Rest 184
   12-12: Renewal 186

THE SPIRAL: The 13th step 195
    Spiral On 197
    Wounded or Wise 200
    Truth, Death, Love 203
    13-1: Truth 204
    13-2: Death 229
    13-3: Love 239

Welcome to Our Campfire

I AM SITTING in a circle of women, way out west in the flat, red dust country of the driest continent on Earth. We are mid-way through a writing workshop, settled into the small shade of an awning, respite from the relentless heat of the sun. An older woman looks up with tears in her eyes, and says: "Does anyone else suffer for small things they did a long, long time ago?" It is one of the bravest questions I have ever heard asked. Nothing was the same from there. We all had tears in our eyes as we remembered. Yes, we suffer for small things we did a long, long time ago.

We wasted neither time nor breath on the stories of our misdeeds. Instead, our attention shifted to the shame we still carried for small unmeant cruelties. We opened our writing hearts to sadness, our own and each other's. Through the tears in each other's eyes and our pens on the page we forgave ourselves.

Nothing more needed to be said, as we wrote our way home.

Write Your Way Home is a book of writing journeys. These journeys are yours for the taking, to be adapted and shaped according to the winds of your own traveller's heart.

It is a book of life. A place to meet the underbelly of the world beneath your waking world. A guide as you meet the personal mythologies that shape your relationships, your health and your wellbeing.

These journeys are for the shattered and the strong; they are for those who are drowning and those with their heads above water. They are for the ones whose world is rocked by forces seemingly beyond their control and those enduring old griefs that have settled in for the duration and outstayed their welcome. They are for the exhausted and the baffled and the disguised and the disgusted, anyone who is diminished and disempowered by the Same . Old . Stories dominating their life. This book is for anyone who longs to understand the energies and forces that influence and overwhelm them, and long to tell a different story.

The writing journeys that follow are for everyone, whether or not you consider yourself a 'writer'.

There are times when you will want to throw the book across the room. *Do it.* There are times you will be confused. *Stay with it.* There are times you will break your heart. *Yes, this is the human way.* It hurts. *Yes it does.* I cannot survive this pain. *Yes you can.*

Like all true journeys, the road ahead will be at times confronting: harsh, puzzling and painful; it will also be liberating: joyful, surprising and empowering. You will meet people I have met and known along *The Write Road*. They could just as easily be people you know in your world. The stories and experiences in these hearts are the stories and experiences that surround you. It was suggested to me I use research subjects, to give credibility to the ideas in this book. That would be to present the faceless as data. For me, in this book, the everyday is enough. You and I are enough. So I have chosen to distil the faces that shone for me, their courage in context.

As you write your way home, write the journeys ahead by hand. Refrain from using a computer. Computers keep you sharp and focussed and drain your energy systems. Handwriting offers you direct connection to the deeper well you seek. It softens you and connects you to a wider world. If you are resisting this direction, there is your starting place. Stalk your resistance and examine your need for control. With a pen.

Write Your Way Home has two journaling sections: The Wheel and The Spiral.

The Wheel is your primary journey home. Once completed, there is a standing invitation for you to begin again. Dive in anywhere.

Use the templates to create your own journeys. Dive in anywhere but by no means skip 12-1: *Embodied Journaling*, where you will meet three of the Intelligences available to you in any moment. This is the foundation of all the work ahead of you. Dive in anywhere but by no means skip Chapter 7: *The Writer's Breath*. This breath is a practice, a life saver; it is there for you anywhere, in any moment, in any situation. If you were a smart phone this breath would be your Google Maps, your know where you are, your I need to find my way out. Dive in anywhere if you like or you must – and know this: for maximum advantage begin at the beginning, let the unfolding chapters lead you; move on if the specific journey is not relevant to you at this time; know it is here for you when you need it.

The second section, The Spiral, raises the courage stakes – exponentially. These journeys are for those who are willing to risk all for revelation. You know who you are. There is no need to tip your life onto the spiral if there is no summons in your heart to do so. You will know whether these journeys are for you.

There are many questions for exploration ahead. Some sections contain a short list of the overview questions, should you prefer to meet the terrain you're about to travel before you dive in. The overview questions are followed by questions designed to lead you on and to and through deep excavation, your Ariadne's thread through the labyrinth.

Whether you write only the turning wheel or psyche demands you take the 13th step onto The Spiral, this book commands you recognise responsibility for your wellbeing. If you have no desire to examine the forces that shape, infuse, control, destabilise, upset and frame your life, walk away now. If you want to things to stay as they are, *better the devil you know*, return this book to the shelf now. If you cannot stand being alone with your thoughts, put this book down, now. Leave it. Walk away. These journeys are not for you.

And if you are a little bit excited by the possibility of peace in your time, a tiny bit curious about the living being you are now and in moments to come, this book is a guide, as gentle and/or as robust as you like, a companion for the journey, an ally in your court.

The foundational philosophy of this book is that health and well-being, like happiness, are not grails to be sought and won, finito, the journey done, happily ever after and all that. Rather, health and well-being are ways of being well. They are ways of being as well as we can be inside all the circumstances of our life and all the days that are ours to have. This book recognises we can grow our capacity for wellness inside the frameworks of our lives, just as they are. As we are. You will also find no promise of 'healing' inside this book. 'Healing' is the endless road, snake oil for our times. *There is no end game.* There is only the day you have. And sometimes the day you have asks no more from you than you lie by the river and rest.

None of what follows is to flatten us into cookie cutter people, all polite and nice and that most excruciating of words when applied to women: 'lovely'. If it is for anything it is to cultivate our world-living adeptness: there is a time to be fierce and strike (empowered women can do this with a flash of fire in their eyes); there is a time to hold your fire (alert, calm-ready); there is a time to make your peace (I have no business here). The point of these journeys is to cultivate the kind of maturity that is stratospherically beyond the reach of saccharine memes that temporarily soothe breaking hearts yet, without action on our own behalf, change nothing.

So let us begin.

In the spirit of the wisdom of the ancient temple of Delphi, the Pythia herself:

"Know yourself."

Chapter 1

THE WRITE ROAD
Your story, your world

There is no greater agony than bearing an untold story inside you.

Maya Angelou

IN MAY 2014, I drove west on a hunch: that Australians living beyond the prayer bead mountains that separates fertile coast from arid inland would like a hand telling their stories. I was a newspaper journalist by trade, a woman in a rapidly changing – some would say dying – industry. Compelled to find work I would enjoy, in environments that were nourishing, expansive, creative, appreciative and professionally fulfilling, I drove to Broken Hill, an urban hub inside the vast red desert known as Outback Australia, and launched *The Write Road*.

After decades of telling stories about others, I would focus on supporting people to tell their own stories, their way. I had no idea how my initiative would unfold, how it would be received or what it would look like. What I needed was work and what I had was an assortment of skills, proficiencies, encounters and explorations that added up to a wide range of experiences I could share.

Over ten years on *The Write Road* I drove 250,000+ kilometres, crisscrossing mountains, plains and rivers, barrelling through the harsh glory of the outback, meeting brave new writers in wooden halls, on remote stations, beside waterholes, inside community centres, delivering hundreds of wellbeing writing workshops to geographically isolated Australians, face to face and online.

In my young adult years I had spent decades scribbling in notebooks on verandahs beneath the traveling moon, on grassy headlands overlooking deep blue oceans, and high upon hilltops among eagles and hang gliders. I know intimately the value of taking time out to rest with the wild world, a notebook and pen on my lap, downloading the day onto paper. It has long been a way of keeping good company, particularly when my children were young and I was the only adult in the house. The writing gave me companionship and intimacy. It put me in touch with deeper realities and momentary truths of my existence. It helped me clarify situations and solve problems and navigate bumpy periods of time. It connected me to the rhythms of Earth: the tides and the winds and the growing grasses. It helped me make peace with each and every day. These days this kind of writing has a name: journaling. And this everyday practice was a foundation stone of *The Write Road*'s wellbeing-through-writing program.

It was through serendipitous encounter that I began this work.

Leaving the coast for Broken Hill I vowed to follow every lead that was offered me. It took three 'you must talk to …'s from generous women before I received the call that would light up the west like a Christmas tree, and launch *The Write Road*. I was in the Broken Hill library, computer and phone plugged into the walls, draft paper plans scattered over the chairs. I answered the phone.

"Are you in Broken Hill?"

"Yes."

"Do you have time for coffee?"

"Yes, when?"

"Now."

Over lemon meringue pie and coffee I met Ellen Day, from the NSW Department of Primary Industries.

"You must run a journaling workshop," she said.

"What for?" I replied. I was puzzled. I had media skills. I had publishing skills. Why would I teach people to sit down with a pen and paper and scribble their thoughts? More to the point, who would see that as worthwhile employment of time and financial resources?

Ellen and I jostled about it for a while. Then she said something that altered the course of my life as surely as a switch on a trainline: "Psychologists and counsellors are always telling us to write down our thoughts but it's confusing. People don't know where to start." Hands down her insistence beat my scepticism and an entire wellbeing writing program was born.

There are as many reasons not to write as there are humans with a longing to write. On *The Write Road* I learned that this is just about everyone. Imagine that, almost every single human being longs to write *something*.

In 2020, curious about how a two-hour writing workshop had such a powerful impact on everyday people's lives, I began work on a PhD investigating the relationship between wellbeing and writing. My research was underpinned by an eighteen-week online writing program, involving both group writing and writing independently between sessions. In brief, my thesis illuminated the following:

- sixteen adults signed up for a writing program. They were, obviously, seeking writing support. However, my research showed the core of their motivations was not writing. There was a deeper motive, and that was the longing for self-aligned expression: *visibility in the world as I know myself to be*
- finding words to match the feelings in our body is imperative to good health and wellbeing. This was a primary finding in my thesis. I called the concept Languaging the Feeling Body through Writing. Feelings are what we feel. They are not emotions. They are not stories about what happened to us. Feelings are in the body, inside our skin. It takes a good deal of attention to find actual feelings and it is enormously

challenging to give them words that align with who we know ourselves to be. Languaging the Feeling Body through Writing is the body speaking for itself. Every writing journey in this book is embedded in this practice

○ although there is an abundance of evidence that shows writing is good for us, there are other factors that contribute to maximising the benefits of wellbeing-through-writing practice. These are headlined by: 1. the imperative of writing outside in nature, and 2. the willingness to act on our own behalf. Importantly, the study found even the most literate of adults may need guidance, encouragement and support to write *what matters to them.*

And that is the purpose of this book.

Write Your Way Home makes available *The Write Road*'s wellbeing-through-writing program in one volume. Why? Because among the myriad wonderful teachings I have received along *The Write Road*, one is a standout: honouring the deep, deep longing of the human spirit to express itself *as we know ourselves to be* is powerful medicine. Astonishingly, for almost all of us, this is predicated on a longing to write, even if only to empty ourselves – our living body – of our too-much story. Why? Because expression is not enough. We are hungry for words that match our experiences of living and our experiences of ourselves. Through writing we can test our words against the page. We can explore, excavate, make sense of our living. We can say too little, say too much. We can empty ourselves of hurt and rage and prepare ourselves to meet challenges ahead, clear-eyed and strong, confident we have words that align with who we know ourselves to be.

Contained in these pages is the unspoken archive of lived experience that walked with me into every workshop, every online course, every retreat on *The Write Road*. Here is the treasure chest I brought to the room. There is no pathway here that I have not walked myself.

These past years I have been privileged to witness incredible transformations in the health and wellbeing of women and men, old and young, the traumatised and the living well, often in just two hours, as they shine a light on their vulnerability and share with others – strangers, friends, family – the vision they've been hiding in their withheld expressive heart. There are almost always tears as we bear witness to the courage it takes to speak dreams almost forgotten and long buried, books and stories and letters home that are begging to be written but held captive in perpetuity by the writer to whom they have been entrusted.

This program has been delivered to people in communities recovering from flood, bushfire, and enduring drought. It has been delivered to teams of health professionals as a resource to sustain their own wellbeing. It has been delivered in retreats for hard working women who would not previously have considered taking a weekend off.

As that early champion of *The Write Road*, Ellen Day, said: "I love these workshops. Everyone walks away two feet taller."

It has been an honour to be the presenter of this work. To share moments of raw and tender courage with other human beings. To work with brave new writers as they summon the strength to transform wellbeing-through-writing practices into public expression, whether that's bringing forth their books and stories, or taking time out to rest with a notebook to download their day. To stand in the wings and watch as new writers become published authors. As troubled souls find solace in a notebook beneath the rising moon. As strangers agree to travel on together, meeting regularly in common purpose with their newfound writing buddies, online and in person, sharing the journey home.

Write Your Way Home has been written for those who long to write, to understand their living, to keep themselves well, to find their way through challenging situations. It is ideal for folk who have no idea where to start. In equal measure, this material has been compiled in response to health professionals who have asked for tips, tools and techniques for introducing wellbeing-through-writing to clients, patients and others in their care, thus incorporating writing as medicine into their professional toolkits.

The rock bottom reality of what I've excavated along *The Write Road* is this: if you have the longing to write, if you have the longing to lay your burdens down, if you have the longing to spill your languaged feeling body onto the page, and you have the means to do so, i.e. rudimentary literacy and access to pen and paper, then you can write. You can write yourself well. You can write your way to the kind of wholeness that makes peace with life.

You can write your way home.

#youcanwrite

Chapter 2

THE POTENT FORCES
The bravest thing you will ever do

EVERY HUMAN life is laden with 'the potent forces'. Regardless of who you are, where you were born, how long you live or even how you live, your life is marinated in the potent forces: surrender, truth, death, courage, love, acceptance, accountability, judgement, resistance, responsibility, expectations, commitment, discipline, entitlement. The potent forces are not emotions, and they are not emotional states. They are things we *do*, actions we take, some naturally, some unnaturally, some willingly and with effort, some unwillingly, some because we should and most because others say we should. None are positive or negative in themselves. All of them invite us to the dance of life.

The potent forces dominate the world into which you were born. They shape every moment of every day of your life. Whether you have danced with them or collided with them, dismissed or embraced them, you have escaped none of them. Whether you know it or not, whether you want to know it or not, the potent forces are with you now, burrowed within, circling and encircling that which you accept and reject, influencing your life, your relationships, your world.

Write Your Way Home is a book of wellbeing writing journeys, and its purpose is twofold:

- to offer you a range of ideas and signposts for writing your way

to good health and sustained wellbeing, whether or not you want to 'be' a writer
- to help new writers establish a regular writing practice that paves the way for the writer within to emerge (don't make the call just yet; the most vehement 'not here to be a writers' have astonished themselves; some have published books).

Either way, whether you want to write your way to wellbeing or 'be' a writer, the potent forces are your raw material. They are your worthy opponents, your faithful allies, sometimes overstepping their mark, at other times having no place on the field as we learn to dance our life dance. At some point along the way we recognise we cannot dance alone, that these forces are our key to mastering life, and we find in them our salvation, delivering the forces a rightful place at our personal altar.

There is no right and no wrong on this writing journey. No shoulds and should nots. No judgement. No censorship.

Write Your Way Home will teach you how to pursue your stories about yourself and others, and to recognise the importance of naming situations and encounters and collisions and events for what they are in your experience. You will learn what is yours and what does not belong to you. You will learn to refocus current cultural obsessions with trauma and its flipside, blame; a crippling duo that prolong wretched agony and immobilise our senses. You will learn to move through and far beyond the stories others tell about you. You will learn to tell yourself the truth, as best you know it in a moment. You will learn to hold your centre. You will learn to be brave. You will grow your courage and with that your confidence. You will find your voice and raise it like a guiltless flag upon which to hoist your languaged visibility. You will write until you are home. You will write your way home.

It's your story. Tell it any way you like.

Crowning our list of potent forces is a trinity of dynamisms that infuse all our interactions. They are fixtures in every human life and they influence *everything*. To ignore this trinity is to glide over the breathless surface of trouble. To face them is to meet your world unblinkered – and give yourself a genuine shot at peace in your time. Peace in *your* human heart is the only chance we have for peace on Earth. When you have raised one then two then three generations of children, you are privileged to observe an astonishing and discomforting reality: the adults we raised have paid zero attention to what we have said over the years; in adulthood our voices are a fly to swat from their thoughts. In reality, they have imbibed our actions and lived to transmit them to another generation, for better and worse, and so on for every generation after that. Peace in ourselves is not only all we need to do, it is the best we can do for the moment we are in, and it is a much, much more effective and challenging path than telling others what to do. Our only task is be ourselves (which is quite distinct from 'my life') and to do that we must make our peace, with ourselves.

The trinity of crowning potent forces that influence our responses to every aspect of our life are Shame, Exile, Forgiveness. These forces are infused throughout this book like mist lying low over gentle landscape.

Shame, the shadow lurking beneath our anger. Shame, our contempt, blame, nothing-good-enough obsession. Shame, the driver of soul-destroying self loathing.

Exile, the fear that we are guilty and stand to lose everything if we act for ourselves (in concert, always in concert); the alternative, a life of struggling to breathe as we outrun the behemoth of stories we have projected onto ourselves and others, and the stories they tell about us.

Forgiveness. Not of others but of self. Not others. Self. Forgive yourself. Forgive yourself all of it. All of it. Forgive yourself and you will find there is no-one else to forgive, no-one left to forgive. What mattered so much you were willing to die for it, die and take others down with you, fades away. Forgive yourself and it's done.

The word 'person/persona' literally means 'the mask through

which we speak'. 'Person/persona' is a deliberate word. A deceptive word whose meaning we have flipped, mistaking the illusion for the one within. Who are you behind the mask? Your shame, we see it anyway. Your exile, terror on the inside. Your forgiveness, in absentia.

Welcome, all of that which is you, welcome.

Welcome to that which you celebrate about yourself, and that which you loathe. Welcome, as you are, as you write your way home.

Chapter 3

WRITING IS A WASTE OF TIME
The case for daydreaming

YOU DON'T have to be a writer – or even want to be a writer – to pick up a pen and put it to paper. So why do it then?

Because like going for a long walk or playing your favourite music or visiting a good friend, writing is great medicine. I have a friend who likes to say 'you don't know what you don't know'. And yet ... *startling truth* ... what you don't know, or refuse to know, or have not taken the time to know, is shaping every moment of every day of your life. It is impacting on your relationships, your sense of purpose, your health, your courage, your confidence. For better and for worse, every moment of every day, your world is influenced by shadowy vulnerabilities, meddling internal voices and old stories moulding your identity and shaping your destiny.

Writing is your key to knowing.

Early on during my years on *The Write Road* two cultural facts emerged:

1. almost everybody wants to write. Isn't that astonishing? Nearly every single one of us longs to write ... *something*
2. almost everyone believes that to take the time to do so would be to 'waste time'. And even if people don't really believe they'd be wasting time, they fear – or they know – other people will think, or tell them, they are 'wasting time', aka 'haven't you got something better to do?'

Wasting time.

Sitting down and doing 'nothing' for a while is now touted as 'wasting time'.

Resting is now 'wasting time'.

Doing what we love, or would love if we had the 'time', is now 'wasting time'.

We have become so vital to our own lives, so busy with our time saving techniques and devices, so consumed by inconveniences small and large, so overwhelmed by the talents of people we admire that far too many of us no longer take time to do the things we love, or would love if we gave ourselves the chance.

Time to rest. Time to daydream. Time to fill the well.

The binary systems of mental and physiological health are growth industries, and yet we tell ourselves *and each other* that we do not have time to do those things we'd love to do more than anything else. Regardless of the myriad pursuits that call to a human heart, underpinning them all, for almost everyone, courses a longing to write, to spill the story from, or tell the story of, our own heart.

And even though hard evidence shows us that in every possible way resting makes us better, still we have 'no time' to laze beneath a tree in the midday heat, and write. No time to sit on the steps while the sun goes down, and write. No time to wander out on the headland, lie back in the morning sunshine and write.

Busy is not only a pain in the neck (literally, and otherwise). It is a lie.

A quick search of the work habits of the world's eminent scientists, artists and thinkers reveals scientist Charles Darwin worked in three ninety minute blocks a day and his day's work was done by lunchtime, after which time he walked in the hills, napped, enjoyed evening meals, read, chatted with friends, went out for coffee (yes, I hear you, his wife and/or housekeeper enjoyed no such luxury). Nonetheless, his work habits were and are not unusual among the subjective collectively-agreed male 'greats'. You may have heard of the famous study by Ericsson and his colleagues, who found it takes ten thousand hours of practice to become world class at anything. Here's what has been largely ignored by those who reference this study for their own purposes: "Deliberate practise," said Ericsson, "is an effortful activity that can be sustained *only for a limited time each day*". Practise too little and you will never become world-class. Practise too much and you increase the odds of being injured, mentally drained, or burned out. To succeed, said Ericsson, people must 'avoid exhaustion' and 'limit practise to an amount from which they can completely recover on a daily or weekly basis'. Completely recover, he said. Completely.

Creativity and productivity (surely they are the same thing?) are not the result of endless work. They are the result of deliberate rest and deliberate work. The reality is that we achieve more when we work less. We are productive when we rest (walk, have coffee with friends, read, nap) *twice as much* as we 'work' (are 'too busy').

Busy is the martyr's badge. Busy is for people who can't organise themselves (ouch!). Busy is for people who are too important to pay attention to love. Busy is for people who are terrified of stillness. Busy is neither more nor less than the everyday demands required to achieve what you yourself have decided you 'have' to have, have to do, have to achieve, have to be.

Busy is not what you have to do in a day but how you do it.

Time is a funny thing. Slow down and it slows with you. Try it some time. Next time you're rushing, slow down. See what happens. Wasting time will make you more productive. It will alleviate stress. It will help you meet the demands of modern living. It will give you the energy you need for the relationships in your life. It will help you access new ideas and new thoughts. It will inspire and motivate and encourage you to do more than you think you can do.

Is she working or is she resting?

Surely, everyone is entitled to sit on their verandah while the sun goes down with a book on their lap and a pen between their fingers, clarifying thoughts, exploring ideas, solving problems, telling stories. It takes courage to override the voices in our head, and all around us, shaming us with the myriad reasons we cannot, should not, must not write the words hammering at our heart and head. It takes a radical act of self-belief to claim our voice and our visibility and be witnessed in the claiming. It takes a personal revolution to place a value on the longing to write so high that we are no longer willing to sacrifice our right to write on the altar of 'wasting time'. And it takes a funny sort of confidence to write not because you're going to be brilliant and not because it may or may not be worth publishing and not because other people might love or hate your story – to write for no other reason than the longing to write is reason enough.

In a radical act of civil disobedience, our task today, and tomorrow and the day after that, is to waste time.

Waste some time. Take your time.

Sit 'idle' during a busy day. Give the gift of wasting time to yourself and set a fine example to others. Take time to connect with your deepest well: sit, dream, rest. From there, who knows, you may just pick up that pen. And write. The words. You. Are longing. To write.

The most powerful thing you can do today is rest. Dare to rest. Dare to waste time. Dare to be inspired.

Empowered people are not 'too busy', 'way busy' or 'crazy-busy'. Powerful people keep their sanity by taking time to meet friends, read, write, daydream. Rest is as vital to their day as breakfast and a good night's sleep.

Dare to be powerful.

Chapter 4

WRITING IS GOOD MEDICINE
The case for writing as a pathway to wellbeing

A WOMAN WALKS into a wooden hall in a small settlement two hundred kilometres from everywhere. She is not young, neither is she old. She is huddled over a walking stick. She is leaning on her husband. Two brief writing workshops later, she leaves the hall. Her eyes are shining. She is walking tall, no longer leaning on her husband. She is swinging her walking stick. What happened in those few hours to change this woman's sense of wellbeing so enormously, at least for a while?

There is ample evidence that while all the creatures of the earth need three things for their survival – air, water, food – human beings have a fourth requirement, and that is to action the longing embedded in the human heart, to create according to our own code. In this woman's case she longed to write. The workshop gave her, at least for a moment, the experience of self-aligned, *languaged* expression.

Yes of course we can survive without painting or taking photographs or writing or crafting the myriad objects a human being may be inspired to create/produce (productivity, see? same thing). Withholding our longing from the world is one thing. However, when we do not allow ourselves the space we need to generate words that align with our internal and external expressions of self, when we deny the longing that can flood the body of a human being, the human spirit will turn on herself. She will contract, she will wither.

Snubbing our longing for self-aligned *languaged* expression will cause the human body to tense, perhaps to become bloated or brittle. Denying ourselves the right to write – to language our living – will eventually overwhelm us. It will harden the heart and sharpen the tongue. It is a silencing, a muting of the human spirit. It is a refusal of self, and this refusal will devour your sense of self in the world. This wilful, frozen, paralytical silencing will haunt and hound and taunt and badger you. It will smother your spirit. And when that happens you will withdraw. You may fall ill. And there's a high probability you will take your silenced choking frustration out on others.

The Write Road offered writing workshops; in fact our currency was courage. Here is what was revealed early as we pioneered this work in the Australian outback:

- writing can enhance and sustain our health and wellbeing
- writing can redefine a person's attitudes in situations of crisis and difficulty
- writing can shape our short- and long-term destiny.

These statements are not theoretical. They are observable, witnessed, witnessable outcomes, and there is research to back them up. In fact the connection between writing, health and wellbeing is well documented. Evidence shows that writing, even the simple act of sharing the words that match our living with only ourselves, can increase our 'sense of coherence', that is, our capacity for managing, comprehending, and making meaning of life's circumstances and events. The sense of coherence concept is rooted in Antonovsky's salutogenesis theory. Antonovsky theorised that human health and wellbeing is not a binary paradigm, that is, we are not either well or sick, as per the pathogenic paradigm that frames western medical systems. Antonovsky's salutogenic theory states that as long as there is breath in our body, we are to some degree well, and that increasing our sense of coherence will strengthen our health and wellbeing as we go about our living in the world. My research demonstrated unequivocally that adults who are offered support to write what matters to them over a sustained period time *will* enhance their capacities and capabilities in and for life – if they are willing to show up to the page.

Wellbeing-through-writing is salutogenic by nature. All *The Write Road* programs are salutogenic in focus. We are interested not in what is not right in a person's world. Our emphasis is the inherent strength and capacity of each individual human being who sits in our circle, all of whom have breath in their body.

Don't take my word for it. There are hundreds of studies that show writing is good for physical, emotional, and mental health and wellbeing, and those who have worked with me and/or have read my research know I do not separate one from the other, that I am concerned only with the whole of the human in the body doing the living. Myriad studies show writing can positively influence immune function, pain, depression, wound healing, and stress. Writing can reduce the number of days we spend in hospital, boost employment prospects after losing a job and increase social interactions. Writing doesn't just make us feel better, in every possible way writing can help make us better.

Writing is medicine. When we write we unburden ourselves of stories we have shouldered for too long, stories that have outlived their purpose, stories that have colonised our bodies, our relationships, our world. Writing releases the story from our blood and our flesh and our bones, thus stilling, at least for the moment, or even a while, the tensions, contractions and despair of repetitive self-talk.

When we write we create an opportunity to language the self-aligned truth of a moment. Even if we are the only ones who hear that truth. Even if we know it is illogical, wide of the mark, unreasonable or downright outrageous. Spilling the words that swirl through the systems of our living body onto the page quickly enables us to comprehend the legitimacy of our feelings, and discern what is actually true from the self-protective, strike-first, whiplash world of 'my truth'. By finding and pinning to the page words experienced by and through the body, we can, if we choose, claim the right to speak clearly on our own behalf. And if we go deeper into this process we will experience the life-changing key to this work: languaging the feeling body in writing. Releasing the story in and of our mind/body/heart/spirit through writing can offer us relief. Languaging the feeling body in writing unburdens us. It releases us from toxic obligation to an old story. It is this process that can, and possibly will, set you free.

As well, when we write we rest. Simple really. What do 'I'm-too-busy' people fail to do when they are hurt or broken or unwell or stressed? They fail to rest. To write we must be relatively still. With or without writing, rest is nourishing.

So there we have it – lay down your burdens, rest, and language for yourself the *actuality* of how you feel and who you know yourself to be. This is self-aligned languaged living. This is the power of writing. Too simple? Try it. Writing may save your life. Hell, it might even save the national health budget.

Chapter 5

THE POWER STORY
The human body, speaking for itself

THIS I LEARNED on *The Write Road*:

Your story is only thing you own. You can lose everything – *every single thing you own* – your home, your relationships, your job, your possessions, your identity. You can lose everything – but you cannot lose your story. Your story is the one thing, the only thing, that no person, no event, no weather, no circumstance can take away from you.

So ultimately, the only thing we truly have, the only thing we truly own, is our story. So how are you going to tell it? There is great personal power to be harnessed from not just knowing your story, but *deciding* how you're going to tell it.

Before that, this:

Underpinning our story is the feeling body. Reality check: that which in the west we frame as 'my truth' is in fact the story we can live with. Yeah? We tell the story we can live with.

Stories have pronouns she and he and they, did and said and didn't do and didn't say – stories are full of other people who (sucks to be us) have their own story-truths, about themselves, about others, about you.

Languaging the feeling body through writing is archaeological in nature and purpose. It is an excavation through layers of hurt and shame and exile and despair and wounded pride and overwhelming helplessness. It is a process that leads us beyond the words and stories others speak to us and of us. It is an interior journey to find the words that match our living as experienced in and by and through the feeling body. It is life beyond story. It has no pronouns. No 'other'. Just words that align with who we know ourselves to be.

This is languaging the feeling body through writing.

The body, speaking for itself.

The Write Road had two foundational workshops: *Embodied Journaling* and *Song of the Soul*. There is a point in *Song of the Soul* when I ask people what they love. *What do you love? What lights you up? What makes you shine?* And do you know no-one, not a single person among the thousands, has ever said they love a material possession. Not cars, not jobs, not computer devices, not phones, not houses, not even homes.

Here's what we love: we love other people, we love music, we love laughter, we love singing and dancing, we love the wild world, we love animals, we love gardens, we love stories, we love making things for ourselves and others.

It is at this point in the workshop the 'wasting time' narrative kicks in, hijacking their story, their world, their life, their wellbeing, their breath, their words, their everything; sacrificing the time they need for what they love to the bewildering debilitating cultural narrative about 'wasting time'.

Here we nudge up against the reason why languaging the feeling body through writing is so important to human living. By taking time to visit the interior body, the world inside our skin, we give ourselves space to make clear decisions about the story we tell about our living. For here is our testing ground: how do you *feel*, in the body, when you tell your story? Any story. Any words you use to speak for or about yourself. How do you feel? Empowered? Strong? Sure-of-self? Undermined? Diminished? Uncomfortable? Anywhere-but-here?

How do you feel in your body?

Reality check: how you feel in your body when you speak for and about yourself, and for and about others, is shaping your life and your destiny.

Chapter 6

THE ONLY QUESTION
The human most brave

IN ALL THE world, there is only one question. Every encounter, every situation, every decision, underpinned by a single question. One question that can change the course of a life and therefore a community in a moment: are you willing?

We are swamped in the messaging of crisis. Advertising, politics, marketing, media. All peddling explosive narratives that shape our ideas about who we are and the myriad forces we have to fear, whilst simultaneously lulling us to sleep with promises they can't keep.

As global health budgets blow out with rising demands for mental health services, we cannot escape the reality that too many of us are being determinedly unbrave. If we can't cope with life now, at a time when our standard of living has never been higher for such a critical number of people, then what do we think our health is going to look like in the days ahead as we navigate these disruptive geopolitical times? What capacity will we have to manage when reality doesn't just bite, it bites hard? If we can't cope now, when so many of us have everything we claim to need and want, ignoring for the moment the stress burdens in our lives through generating what we claim to need and want, how are we going to meet the challenges ahead, when the forests burn and the rain doesn't come and the cities freeze and the islands sink and whopping waves wipe the shoreline clean and the big water rolls into town not once every hundred years but regularly and often? Global climate disruption isn't coming, it's upon us. Disruption to global supply chains isn't coming, it's upon us. War isn't just coming to the fringes of Europe, it's upon us. These are challenging times and there are more challenges ahead. If we are unwilling to take the reins now for the health and wellbeing so essential to navigating our times, then when?

We in the westernised world have raised children who want for nothing. Yet they are beset with 'mental health' issues. Do we see the irony here? In our industrialised lives most of us create nothing for ourselves. Not with our own hands. We want without taking responsibility for any part of that which we claim to want, other than the consumer transaction at the end and even then too often we are left indebted to big money. We don't make. We buy. We post Facebook memes of concern for the price others pay for our incessant wanting yet purchase that same product. The bed we sleep in, the plates we eat from, the trinkets on our shelves, the clothes on our back. We contribute nothing more than our endless wanting to their creation, offer zero accountability for the ensuing mess that's created on our behalf, then burst a boiler at banks and corporate profiteers because in reality we couldn't afford what they facilitated us to buy (see? lulling us to sleep with promises they/we can't keep).

Everything most of us have is mass produced. It has no inherent value. Everything is done for us. Yet we have 'no time'. We bleat at governments to 'do something' in the belief that we ought not be required to give up anything for our demands. Plastic bags at the supermarket don't count. Those corporate mega-profits were/are stockpiled on the backs of our endless wanting. Our collective stress, our ill-health, other people's ill-health, our children's ill-health, other people's children's ill-health, the water crisis, the planetary crisis, the arms crisis – it was, is, all for our wanting. I know right, there is no crisis ... until it comes for us: you, me, us.

What has this got to do with writing for wellbeing?

Priorities. We claim we want to be well yet it is as if we are determined to be unwell. Determined to worry ourselves sick. Determined to outsource responsibility for our lives. Determined to cling to lifestyles that burden us and belief systems that shatter our spirits. Determined to buy exotic stuffed animals while we bulldoze living specimens into oblivion. Determined to be broken. Determined to take our hands off the wheel. Determined to avoid the longing that is beating inside each and every human heart. Determined to live for an impossible future without regard for the one day we actually have.

A while ago I was privileged to spend time with UK writing for wellbeing practitioner Roz Mascall, when she made the kind of throwaway line that doesn't leave a wrestling heart alone.

"A mask needs an audience," she said.

Simple, really.

A mask needs an audience.

We can learn a lot in a flash.

The point at which we are unmasked is the same point at which we are no longer performing, for ourselves or others. It is the point at which we are stripped of stories imposed upon us. The point at which we no longer ascribe to external factors that identify us to an unseeing world, such as descriptions of/pronouncements about our personality, status updates about our work, holidays, relationships, broken or forsaken health, and so on. If no-one is witnessing our situational identity, trauma or pain does it exist in the same way? Does it exist at all?

Next to breathing, writing is the most accessible health and wellbeing resource available to people in a literate society. Writing is revelation. It offers clarity. It is a self-empowerment device. It is medicinal. It's like running through a dark house turning on the lights.

Writing for our health and wellbeing demands courage. Courage to overcome the voices and demands of others. Courage to take time out from feeling overwhelmed. Courage to appear to be idle. Courage to rest. Courage to relinquish control *for ten minutes*. Courage to show up for our health and wellbeing. Courage to allow the gift of self-aligned languaged expression in the world. Courage to do what we love. Even if you never learn to love writing, there's a high probability you will love where it can lead you, which is, straight through the open doorway of your own longing.

The startling reality is you cannot outsource your wellbeing.

If you will not decide to be well, all the experts in the world cannot help you. Of course there is help to be had on the outside, but they can only work with you, they cannot do it for you. No-one but you can give you courage, yet without it you will remain determinedly unwell. No-one but you can give you time (reality check: you have all the time in the world, *you actually do*). Besides, why would others give you what you are unwilling to give yourself? Why *should* others give you what you are unwilling to give yourself? These are not rhetorical questions. Answer them. Grab a pen and paper and answer them.

Acting on the longing of the human spirit for self-aligned languaged expression takes courage. Actioned courage makes us strong. Brave. Robust. Resilient. Ready. Actioned longing is an act of radical self-possession. It teaches us the difference between heightened senses (sensible) and stress. No longer unhappy.

We humans like to think other people are hard on us. It is nothing compared to how merciless we can be on ourselves. Emptying your body of the burdens it carries by spilling them onto the page, there to burn when you're ready or stay bound-as-witness to your living, is more than an act of courage, it is an act of love. Stepping forward to write the story you've been longing to write, even if it is only your small story-of-the-moment, for your eyes only, is more than an act of courage, it is an act of love. Here we find the humans most brave, the ones unmasked. The ones who exist with *and* without an audience. The ones who are willing to write because they long to write. The ones who are willing to shine for no other reason than to honour their longing to shine, to live in the world as they were born to live in the world.

The question is: are you willing?

Are you willing to be well? Are you willing to live for what you claim to 'want'? And if not that then what? What are you willing to live for? And if your answer is not for you but for others, why not you too? Why are they worthy and you are not? Are you willing to give up imagined fears and other people's stories about you and your living? Are you willing to unmask yourself *to yourself*? Are you willing to stare down shame? (Oooo, that's brave.) Are you willing to overcome your fear of exile? (Yep, that's brave too.) Are you willing to forgive yourself? (Oo-ee, here is love.)

Are you willing?

Chapter 7

THE WRITER'S BREATH
When all else fails, breathe

WRITING IS THE most accessible health and wellbeing tool available to people in a literate society. Before writing, breathing. When all else fails, breathe. Sometimes a single breath is all that's left to do. Then the next breath. A deep breath anchors us to our body, anchors our body to Earth. Literally. Just as the great force of electricity must be 'earthed', so too human energy must 'ground' in order to live well.

Walk tall, walk straight and look the world right in the eye. This was a song about a straight spine and a deep breath. You can look the world in the eye only when you are inside your skin. Breathing is your ticket in. Breathing gives you access to an infinite swash of information. It's your 'open sesame'. Breathing helps you see more, hear more, gather more intelligence. Breathing renders you strong, makes you brave, holds you true.

The Writer's Breath is your ally, at all times, in all situations. *The Writer's Breath* is your passport to writing fluidly, easily, to pouring your daily world onto an empty page, to downloading stresses and navigating your way through challenging situations. *The Writer's Breath* is not mindfulness, and it is not meditation. *The Writer's Breath* is the writer's breath.

You can access *The Writer's Breath* in a blink, at a contentious meeting or a family debacle or mired in heavy traffic. When someone or something throws you out of your own orbit, breathe. Come inside. Slow the wobble. Take up residence on the inside of your skin. Stand (or sit) tall. Look the world in the eye. Put your hands on the wheel. And use *The Writer's Breath* to steer yourself out of an onerous or dangerous situation.

Or use it to write your way home.

Getting to *The Writer's Breath*

The Writer's Breath is a practice – literally, something to be practised. Sure, you can avoid it. Give it no value. That's fine. Know it is here for you when or if you decide you'd like more centralised power in your life than you currently employ or enjoy.

Most of us spend very little time consciously inside our body, let alone take up permanent residence. It can be incredibly difficult to come 'home'. Body/abode: home-home, same word. Coming home can feel unsafe. Tortured. *Anywhere but here.*

For each and every writing journey offered in this book we will call upon *The Writer's Breath*. Adapt this practice as you will. You will learn to access it in an instant. Make it your own. Whatever form it takes for you, a breathing practice that connects you unequivocally to Earth, inside your skin, is key to accessing deeper realms and knowledges of your being and the myriad situations unfolding around you. It is your passport to responsibility for your own wellbeing, your source of increased personal power and peace in your time.

If you're up for it, let's begin.

The Writer's Breath

Feet on the ground. *The Writer's Breath* always starts by coming to Earth. Feet on the ground. Come to Earth. Ground. Close your eyes. And breathe. Feel where your feet connect to the ground. Focus on your feet. If your feet are on a floor then beneath the floor is dirt, red brown black yellow grey dirt. Ground. Feet flat to the floor. Below the floor, Earth. Connect.

CHAPTER 7

Sit up straight. Spine straight. As you align your bones, let gravity do its thing with your flesh. If you cannot sit then lie down. However you must hold your body, let your body come to ground. If you cannot put your feet on the ground then your spine or whole of body: beneath you your bed, beneath your bed the floor, beneath the floor, Earth. Whether you sit or lie, take a deep breath through the centre of your chest. Take that deep breath through the centre and breathe, through the centre. Breathe through your heart. All your awareness on the breath, coming and going through the heart; a wave on the shore, tide in, tide out, breath in, breath out. Feet on the ground. Earth below. Below your feet a planet. A massive sphere of molten rock and fire (*yes, really*). All that energy, breathe up from the centre of Earth, up through your beating heart. Breathing up, up through the soles of your feet. Up through your legs. Breathing up through your spine. Breathing through the heart, breathe it up. Breathe it up. Through your legs, up your spine. Up your spine and out the top of your head, bursting into the vast space above you.

Sky. Blue sky. Night sky. Clouds. Stars. Sky above. Earth below. You are the channel. Breathing through your heart, up from the Earth, through your body and out through the top of your head. Sky above. Vast sky. Open space. Breathe the sky bodies down through the top of your head into your heart. Stars, moon, planets, comets, meteoroids, black holes. Breathing sky. Earth below sky above breathing. Life force all around you.

Your skin. The world around you nestles up against your skin. Sunshine. Warmth on your skin. Breeze. Wind. Damp of night. Breathing through your skin. Skin. The world around you. Your skin breathing time with the rivers, trees, mountains, rolling hills, stretching plains, breathing them in, breathing through your skin now. Your skin breathing. Life force all around you. And all the while your breath is running through the central channel that is your spine, your heart.

Eyes closed, you can no longer tell where you end and the world around you begins. Breathing deeply. Eyes closed. There is as much space between the cells in your body as there is between celestial bodies in the universe, relatively speaking (pure science). Breathe the spaces. Life force all around you. Life force running through you. Space inside you. There is a mystery force in the universe. A dark wind, yet to be defined (check it out). The dark wind is running through you. It almost never touches a single cell in your body. Breathe the spaces between your cells. Ride the dark wind.

And come inside. Inside. Breathing now on the inside of your body, on the inside of your skin, your blood running, your bones solid, the flesh of your beating heart falling its gentle way to Earth. Breathing. On the inside. Inside your feet, right here breathing with the bones inside your toes. Your hands, the bones in your fingers. Breathing, through the heart inside your ribcage. Inside your ribs. All your awareness below the neck. Breathing on the inside. Inside with your life giving organs. Inside your arms. Inside your legs. Inside your chest. Inside your pelvis. Breathing.

Breathing. Knitting your soul/spirit/lifeforce within to the inside of your skin. Breathing. Every cell. Expanding. Opening. Receiving the life force energy that is all around you, running through you, riding the breath, riding every breath.

Breathing. Spine straight. Sitting tall. On the inside. And now, look. Look. Hold your centre. Breathing through the heart. Look from the inside, out through your eyes. Look the world right in the eye.

You are ready. Ready to begin. Whatever it is you are doing, do it from here, from the centre, from the inside.

Chapter 8

THE TURNING TIMES
The lunar art of rest in a busy world

ALL OF LIFE IS subject to the laws of rhythm. There are the obvious rhythms: sun up, sun down, moonrise, moonset. The moon grows large, then darkens and hides, only to rise and swell again, giving us our tides. The sun lights our days, longer in summer, shorter in winter, giving us our seasons. These are great sacred rhythms of which we are all a part, whether we know it or not, whether we want to know it or not, we are part of the rhythm of life.

There was a time before time. A time when all of life, human and non-human, was deeply embedded inside the rhythms of our wild spinning universe. A time when there was all the time in the world. A time when there was no concept of separation of human from the wild world. Humans in modern societies, the tick tock of the clock strapped to their wrist, no longer move with the ancient rhythms. And yet the rhythms are with us still, cyclical, spiralling, expanding, influencing.

Fact check: time does not exist. It is a fabrication. An imposition. It is not real. Sunday exists only because many of us agree it exists. In fact there is no such thing as Sunday, or Monday. Thursday, mmm nope, doesn't exist. Calendar dates are a concept. It was 2020 because we said it was. In fact, 2020 was 1441 in the Islamic calendar. 1469 according to the Armenians. The Baha'i said it was

176-177. The Balinese 1941-42. The Buddhists 2563. The Byzantines 7528-7529. The Chinese Earth Dog-Earth Pig/4716-4717 or 4656-4657.

Days and dates and times have meaning because we collectively agree they do, and we are buckling under the weight of that illusory meaning. For here is our busy story, our 'no time' story. Here is our crazy. Our crisis. Our crises. Entrenched in a rigid structure that in reality has no specified purpose other than to coordinate us coming together in a timely way. That's what it's for. Tick tick tock. Rush. No time. Past, present, future. Hurry. No time. Regrets. Hopes. Delays. Your life beating time to years, days, hours, minutes, seconds. Your beautiful days, regulated by digitised numbers and ticking hands.

There's no such thing as time. We made it up. It is a story. An artifice. So when you say you 'don't have time' you're absolutely correct. The alternative is to say you have all the time in the world, which is also absolutely correct.

Many years ago I ran a media training business on the Gold Coast. There came a morning when I arrived at work to find I'd said yes to far too many commitments and they were converging on this particular Tuesday. I had the proverbial snowball's chance in hell of meeting those deadlines.

After prolonged moments of panic, I rebelled. I decided that instead of panicking, I would do only one thing and I would do it well. When that one thing was done, if there was time I'd do another. I would do one thing at a time. I would work slowly. I would work deliberately. I would not think about anything else but the task at hand. I would not sweat what I would not be able to finish that day.

I selected my first task. Completed it. Moved onto the next. Completed that. I worked my way through my list. By lunchtime I was sitting across the road from my office on the grassy headland watching the waves roll in, thinking 'how did I get here, at this time, on this day?' I have experimented with time ever since and here is what I have learned: time is fluid. Throw away the clock and time does not exist. You can put time to work for you and here's how:

- when you find yourself rushing, slow down (*it feels wicked!*)
- when there's too much to do, go slower (*I dare you*)
- focus only on the task at hand and give it all of your attention (*commit: turn off your phone, shut down your emails, close the internet connection on your computer if it's not necessary to the task*)
- do not waste your energy giving anything else a single thought (*if you have to be somewhere else 'on time', set an alarm and forget about it*).

And here's why it works: it works because you will move with the rhythm of the day. In my case I worked with the rising time. At the rest point of the day, sun high, my day's work was done. And even if my tasks had not been completed, it would have served me well to rest with the resting time and, once rested, applied a slower, less driven energy to my work in rhythm with the closing of the day.

There's no such thing as time. Don't take my word for it. Ask a physicist. No matter how regimented your daily life to the ticking hands of the clock, every single day there are times available to you where you can access powerful energies of and from the wild spinning universe around you – *if* you are willing to rest, tune in and receive what is yours by birthright. These are the turning times. Your invitations to quietly align with a rhythm greater than your own clockwork life. Think about this for a moment: the reality of the massive forces and energies of which we are an integral part: the sun, a burning star, Earth: a massive ball of rock and fire thinly wrapped in a layer of blue, green and brown, littered with living life-forms, *turning*.

Earth, turning. Sshhhh, listen. Can you hear our planet turn? What a force. You can certainly see it, right there in the rising sun burning off the damp of night. These are big forces to work against. Bigger than you and me to be sure. Are you going to work with them or against them? Isn't it hilarious that we humans think we can impose our will on a day? *No time, no time, too busy.* Go on, laugh. We are funny. You, me, we are not exempt from the laws of rhythm. Even our small lives have rhythm, times when we are strong, times when we are vulnerable, times we must withdraw until we are strong, only to rise again.

Days have rhythm. Sun up, sun down. Except the sun neither rises nor sets. It is the Earth that spins the day and night. A year in 'time' is in reality one Earth revolution of the sun. The Earth, a planet, our home, traveling around the sun, tilting this way and that, ever and always re-turning us to summer, autumn, winter, spring. Seasons of life. A time to sow and a time to reap. A time to withdraw and a time to rise. The traveling moon, now dark, now full. There is no dark side of the moon. There is only the moon in synchronous orbit between the sun and Earth. The full moon the Earth between moon and sun. Rhythm. The dance of life. Outside time. Beyond human intervention or control.

As a regular part of every day, tune in with the turning times. This practice will open your senses and deliver you access to full bodied information, knowledge, intelligence and creative solutions to impossible moments. Wisdom. Health. All that is asked from you is that you surrender to the rhythms of the wild spinning universe flowing around you and through you.

Sit with a notebook and pen on a verandah, in your bed by a window, under a tree, beside a river, a single weed growing through a crack in the footpath will do. Sit with the coming dawn, the dying light, the night sky, the traveling moon. Anywhere that puts you in direct line with a wild rhythm greater than your own. Sit, tune in, gather your thoughts.

And write your way to wellbeing. Download your busy. Let

the passing light and the growing night sweep your stresses away. Take back the enormous psycho/physiological power you have surrendered to the imposition of time. Right now you have all the time in the world. Every moment of every day, all the time in the world.

Chapter 9

TRY ON THE ORANGE
Would not, could not, should not, do not

MANY, MANY years ago I was invited to try on an orange shirt. I did not like orange. I did not wear orange. As far as my story goes I had never worn orange. Kicking up dust all the way to the change room I threw on the orange shirt – and turned to the mirror to find I was alight. The orange had lit me up. Orange was my colour.

This journey towards claiming languaged self-alignment of your living will compel you to action and invite you to travel roads you'd really rather avoid. It will encourage you to defy the one inside your head that 'will not' take action on her own behalf.

This journey will insist you try on the orange. It will demand you step forward for the longing in your heart. Stepping forward for your longing is possibly the bravest thing you will ever do. I know right? Terrifying. Claiming your birthright. Terr-i-fy-ing.

The good news is you are never given truthful purpose without also being given the personal resources you need to honour it and get on with it. However. There is a however. Stepping forward to claim the languaged beating heart of your life's longing *will* unleash a riot of ragged voices raging at you with their sticks and stones and shields of common war.

Except, brave ones, except – except now we confront the hater within.

The resister. The one who under no circumstances will exchange curiosity for resistance. The one who will refuse to open to new ideas. The one who wants a fight. S/he is a chameleon, fallaciously given credence in our modern spiritual age as 'my inner truth'. *Do not mistake her for your psyche/soul, calling.* Resistance is a killer and it is your emerging deepest longing that it's after.

Write Your Way Home is an invitation to surrender that resistance. To deny and defy the one on the inside forcing you to flee. To challenge the angry one within intent on her belief that she knows better. To make visible your self-sabotage. To expose the challenges standing between you and the truth of your existence. To burn in the fires of your own internal rage. To rake through the ashes of your fire and root out new ways to erupt the bitter war within. To be braver today than you were yesterday. And try on the orange.

There is an old tale credited to the First Nations people of Turtle Island, known to us as North America. Some say it is Cherokee. Some say Lenape.

The story goes like this:

A tribal elder is teaching her grandson about life:

"A fight is going on inside me," she said to the boy.

"It is a terrible fight and it is between two wolves. One is evil – she is anger, envy, sorrow, regret, greed, arrogance, self-pity, guilt, resentment, inferiority, lies, false pride, superiority, and ego.

"The other," she said, "is good – she is joy, peace, love, hope, serenity, humility, kindness, benevolence, empathy, generosity, truth, compassion and faith.

"The same fight is going on inside you, and inside every other person too."

The grandson thought about this for a moment and asked his grandmother:

"Which wolf will win?"

The old woman replied: "The wolf you feed."

A word on privacy

Are you free to journal in the sanctuary of your home? Maybe you are, maybe you aren't. Stepping forward to claim the self-aligned passing truth of you does not automatically entitle others to read or share or know that passing truth. Perhaps you long to write your way home but fear others finding your journal. Fear them finding it, reading it. Fear exposing your downloads and stressful thoughts and random purgings to people who are blind to the need for privacy and/or careless and/or vindictive. Or perhaps you are terrified of dying and leaving angry words, momentary irrationalities, transitory emotions on a once-blank page as your legacy. I know I am. I know many people are.

You have a right to write. A right to choose your pathway to wellbeing. A right to explore your thoughts and ideas and opinions, reasonable and outrageous and downright explosively fuck you, in the privacy of your own heart. To say otherwise is to silence to yourself. To choke yourself. To sacrifice your wellbeing on the altar of someone else's fears and toxic terrors.

There are two issues here: the absence of privacy and the possibility of leaving the journal behind if, without warning, your life is done.

Both are easily addressed.

If you do not, or fear you do not, have privacy at home, find a place you can make your own and write there: a park, a riverbank, a patch of wild weeds. If you seek privacy beyond your home there are ways to create a nourishing world in which to write, even if it means stopping on your way home from the shopping and sitting in your car with the sunshine pouring in, or down by the river shrouded by a curtain of rain.

The point is your right to write. So write. It might be the bravest thing you do for now, or the bravest thing you ever do. What matters is you take that step. What matters is you unburden your body from the stories it carries. What matters is you feel the lightness that comes with telling yourself the self-aligned languaged truth of the moment, with navigating challenging waters, with finding solutions, with writing your way home.

And if you don't want your mind dump hanging around, write it out and tear it into tiny shreds and leave it in a bin. Or burn it. Write and burn. Write and burn write and burn write and burnwriteandburnwritean …

A woman who came along to a journaling workshop emailed me later to say she had spent seven nights straight in her back yard with a bottle of wine and a small fire eliminating a story that had taken root in her bones. Writing until she was done. Burning as she wrote. Writing her way home.

There's no need to bottle things up ever again. Did you catch the language there? Don't bottle your story. Let it flow. Undam the river that is your life force. Let your thoughts run. Unleash your stories. Free yourself from the burdens you carry.

And if you fear that once you start you'll never stop that's okay too! I have written for an entire day on headlands and in forests, sun up to sun down, filling notebooks with an old story that was creating toxic rubbish in my cells. And so what if you're unreasonable about people? It's still okay to write it. You may know they were doing the best they could in the situation. That doesn't change the story you hold and the pain and the trouble that has lodged inside you.

It's a story. It's not real. Release it. Say everything. About yourself included. *Woulda shoulda coulda didn't failed.* Give yourself permission to SAY EVERYTHING, unapologetically and without censor, blurt it out to the page and get it out of your system, honouring your need to tell the story as it is in this moment.

It's your story, you can tell it anyway you like.

And then stand by for the miracle: the story will change as it leaves you, and a new story will come.

Re-turn

Journaling will almost always take you into the past, to the old stories embedded in your bones. This is unavoidable, as it is the old stories whispering like autumn leaves returning to Earth that make up the compost of our lives.

If you take up writing as a pathway to wellbeing it is imperative that you end your journaling sessions by returning to the present. To the world you inhabit now. To the people who are with you at this time.

The point of journaling is to move the old stories on, not give them new oxygen. Recognise that at times the old stories may rise suddenly to claim you, striking swiftly again and again until you've finally had enough of their grip on your life and you are ready to move them on – and this can take time. It is imperative therefore that after your journaling session you take responsibility for returning to the present with as little baggage as you can. That you settle your bill with the past on each visit.

Always end your writing for wellbeing sessions with a positive note, such as:

List three things I love in my life. 1, 2, 3. Why do I love them?

What am I looking forward to tomorrow? Why?

Know what you love.

Here. Now. Return.

And write your way home.

WRITING THE WHEEL
12 writing journeys for life

Please subdue the anguish of your soul.
Nobody is destined only to happiness or to pain.
The wheel of life takes one up and down by turn.

Kālidāsa

THE WHEEL OF LIFE

THE WHEEL of Life has long been a foundational symbol of the rise and fall of human existence. The Celts, the Tibetans, the First Nations tribes of Turtle Island/North America, the Aztec civilisation of Mesoamerica, Tony Robbins and other corporate gurus of the new age – the concept of a wheel of life has emerged in myriad cultures over thousands of years and is with us still.

It is employed as a tool for recognising life's balance sheet, a guide to living artfully, a reminder that change is a constant in all human lives and what rises will turn on the wheel of life to fall and rise again. In an uncertain world we can be sure of one thing: the wheel will turn.

There are twelve writing journeys ahead. Twelve is the number of completion. The turning of the wheel. The beginning again. Twelve the months in a year, the hours on a clock, the days of Christmas, court cards in a deck, major keys in western music, jurors in a court room, houses of astrology, knights at Arthur's table, disciples at the Christ's supper. The Norse, Hindu, Greek, Christian, Arabic and Hebraic cultural, religious and mathematical traditions all feature systems based on twelve.

Here is where the work on your wellbeing-through-writing journey begins, rubber to the road. Until now we have been rolling over the surface of the ideas contained in this book. If you have come this far, you are no longer off the hook. There is work to be done. Too easy for me or anyone else to say 'just do it' and voila! all will be right on your world. It's not enough and you know it. You have to live it.

Theory or practice? The fly-by-nighter's passing high or disciplined ongoing courageous action. What will you choose?

However or whatever you feel about what is going on in your life it is a story. Situations happen. People get in your way. It is you who gives events meaning. That meaning is your story. A tale. A yarn. A story you can tell myriad different ways. A story that will shape who you are if you tell it often enough and long enough. A story that will snare you inside a myth of your own making once others pick up its thread and run with it. You will become your story. They will make sure you do. *This is who you are.*

The story is a trap. It is where shame takes root and fear of exile backs you into a corner and instead of forgiving yourself and telling a new story you go on the offensive enlisting others to play attack roles knowing all the while that if you can see your shame, then they can see it too, and so we go, around on the wheel of life.

There's only one reason we do not greet life's challenges with love and a smile and dance, and that is the pain in our bodies. The shame that causes us to wither and want to die, the exile we fear from tribal heart and hearth, the self loathing that comes from the absolute refusal to forgive not others but ourselves. It is you who is carrying this story. You who are peddling it, you who is using it for your own seditious purposes.

Cut off its oxygen. Give it no more fuel. Just walk away? Yes. Modern psychology would have you dredge through it. I'm a Gordian Knot kinda woman. Cut it. Swiftly. There. Done. *But this happened to me.* Yes. It did. How willing are you to confront the story you tell about it? To leave it here on the road? To walk on without it?

So Alexander the Great arrives at the palace of Gordium in the ancient kingdom of Phrygia, to find an oxcart tied to a post by an intricate knot, and a prophecy: whoever untangles the knot is destined to rule all of Asia. Well we know what Alexander wanted. He struggled this way and that to loosen the knot without success. So Alexander drew his sword and sliced the knot in a single stroke, releasing the ox cart and winning his prize.

The stories that have entangled you and enmeshed you in the fears and insecurities of others are your Gordian Knot. The impossible burdens you carry in your heart, Gordian Knot. Your troubles, your shame, your hidden arsenal of self loathing, your Gordian Knot. Your burden to carry, your whip with which to control the lives of others, your shame weaponised so you can pass on your legacy of fear.

Your story is your personal kingdom, your life, your Phrygia, your all of Asia. Will you hold to the myth or slice through it? Will you tie yourself in knots over old stories perpetuated by the telling and retelling, imprisoned by time and making trouble, real or imagined? Or will you release the story from your body in a single stroke. Lighter. Taller. Free of heart. Done.

What's it to be? The myth of your own making or resolution?

12-1 EMBODIED JOURNALING
You know more than you think you know

EVERY HUMAN being carries stories. Big stories, little stories, old stories, new stories, ancient stories, nation stories, family stories. Every single time you have an emotional reaction to anything at all during your day it takes up residence inside your body, there to become a product of memory and imagination, and another story works its way into your bones. The story may build on previous stories, loading one upon the other until the weight becomes so much, too much, overmuch to bear. The story may be a fresh story, staking out new territory inside you like ants after melting honey.

So here's the deal: you can allow stories to colonise your beautiful body being or you can catch them out before they land. The most accessible, powerful, cost-effective tool available to you to do this is journaling. Put simply, journaling is scribbling down what's on your mind. More artfully, *Embodied Journaling* is the gentle craft of releasing stories from your body. And the gift? In five minutes, ten minutes, an hour, whatever time you have to give, you will begin to access greater knowledge, insight and wisdom than you thought possible.

You will be calmer.

You will be smarter.

You will meet challenges with focus and intent.

Journaling will settle you. Refresh, renew and replenish you.

Journaling will fill the well that ten minutes ago you thought was dry. It will make way for your dearest, freshest, most contented self to rise and claim her rightful place in your day, your evening, your life.

We know writing doesn't just make us feel better, that in every possible way it makes us better. Journaling is your ticket to everyday wellbeing, a powerful tool for clarifying thoughts, solving problems and establishing clear pathways forward as you pursue family, life and work goals and navigate choppy waters during challenging times. We all know what's like to anticipate situations in everyday life, where we foresee a conversation or meeting that we fear – or know – will be awkward or difficult. It might be troubles with a neighbour, a family member, a work colleague. Journaling is a powerful tool for preparing ourselves for these encounters, increasing your chances of saying what you wish you'd said. By taking the time beforehand to meet the myriad forces, energies and stories you bring to the situation, you are positioning yourself to take responsibility for eliminating your piece of the bitter story, empowering yourself to put your focus right where you need it to be: on the best possible outcome for you. And if you can go so far as to forgo your need for an enemy, you will lead the way to the best possible outcome for everyone. Peace in this place.

A while back I ran an *Embodied Journaling* workshop in a nowhere town in the middle of the vast flat country in the west. A young Aboriginal woman joined us. She was thin, seven months pregnant, the baby soon-to-arrive like a basketball on her belly. She had already lost two children to community services. She was in need of a great deal of support. She was the only Indigenous woman among seven white women in the workshop.

At the end of the session, as everyone stood to leave, she piped up: "I would like to read my writing." I looked around at the leaving women and invited those who needed to leave to do so, indicating with a nod that those who stayed would be staying for as long as this took. To their eternal credit everyone sat down. And so it was that this somewhat broken young woman exacted the attention of seven sure-of-place non-Indigenous women and shared her private journey.

Please, picture that scene.

This young woman had lost just about everything there is to lose. She had claimed new ways to tell her story.

Later that week, she said to her support worker: "I have never felt as calm as I have since that workshop."

This is the power of visibility. The power of claiming our right to raise our voice. The empowerment of speaking our self-aligned languaged experience.

The power of telling your self-aligned story.

Journaling is a way of building a relationship with yourself. It is a means for uncovering the greatest personal power available to you in a moment. If you are brave enough to tell yourself the truth of the moment, even as you know 'the truth' changes the moment you tell it, this new knowing will empower you and prepare you to meet life as it is, regardless of what life presents to you.

Journaling ensures you address the heated emotion of the encounter before you become embroiled in it. Journaling clears old stories from your field, including and especially from your physical body, so you are strong and centred in and for the coming storm. Journaling equips you with knowledge, insight and wisdom to know not just what you want, but how to language what you want, before you enter the encounter. It also readies you with a strategy that has the potential to move everyone forward, productively. If you're tired of the war, or wish to avoid one altogether, journaling is your secret ally.

Human beings transmit energy. It's what we do. It doesn't matter how vehemently someone wants to tell you they're fine, if they're not fine you know it. We transmit, peace, hostility, rage, delight. We are transmitters. Journaling helps us create clear signals before we enter challenging situations.

When you take time to express yourself in the seclusion of your own world, letting the pen run wild with your thoughts, including the deep-seated crazy, illogical, hostile emotions that lurk in our systems ready to pounce whether or not they are relevant to the current situation, as you name everything there is to be named, without judgment or fear of judgment, you are in a position to familiarise yourself with your fears, explore options for the way forward and, most importantly, give yourself the opportunity to clarify the outcome that is most desirable before you enter the encounter.

Journaling will help you maximise the potential of every moment in your everyday life. As long as you have a notebook and pen with you, in your bag, in the car, beside your bed, this marvellous tool is available to you everywhere.

It's your story. You decide how it goes.

The Three Intelligences

There are many intelligences available to a human being, wellsprings of wisdom and sources of information on standby, ready to aid your responses to situations, events, occurrences, and encounters with others. *Embodied Journaling* teaches you how to access three of them, in any moment, in every situation, intelligences that give you immediate access to clarity, relief, insight, wisdom and 'the right thing to do'.

The Three Intelligences is a process. It is the foundation stone of all the writing journeys that follow in this book. You will call on this process again and again and again. Eventually, it will be accessible to you at will, with or without the availability of a pen, regardless of the situation or who else is with you in the room.

With a nod to the trinary that frames modern westernised new age living, the three intelligences are: mind, body, spirit. As you practice this process, you will find they merge, that in the end your breathing will knit you/them together and there will be only one intelligence and that is 'source', and it is available to you through no-separation: mindbodyspirit-psyche-breath.

Access to The Three Intelligences is inseparable from *The Writer's Breath*. Hand in glove. They are a practice. To be *practised*. They are your potential. To be *practised*. They are a source of power. To be *practised*.

Embodied Journaling

Yes, journaling is a tool available to you at any time for relief, clarity and insight. Used optimally, it as an everyday practice that invites you to make peace with your day and/or prepares you to face your day. There is no 'right' setting and no 'right' time. There are however best practice times that maximise the benefits for you. These would be the 'turning times' outlined in an earlier chapter and they include sunrise, sunset, moon rise, bedtime; moments of transient peace that invite you to tune in to the rhythm of the universe spiralling around you. Find your resting place, where you can sit quietly and watch the world around you shift in the light: on the verandah steps, through a window, on a nearby headland, in bed looking out a window, by a river, beneath a tree. These are the times and places that enable us ready access to our deepest well.

Your tools for *Embodied Journaling* are a notebook and pen. You may also like to include a box of crayons, for as you begin to understand this process the crayons are a particularly handy way of expressing emotions and thoughts that have been written over and over and we do not need to write again but we do need to eliminate from our energy systems – again! The crayons are a fast track to repetitive expression, a shorthand means for giving thoughts colour and form. They are also a wonderful starting place for transitioning from your busy workday world into the journey that awaits you on the empty page.

There are nine exercises below, to be explored, shaped, adapted to your writing and journeying direction. They are an entire session if you so choose, to be worked through consecutively. Equally, they are random ideas to be called upon depending on the needs of the moment.

Shall we begin?

Exercise 1: Tuning in

Close your eyes. The moon, where is the moon? Where is the moon in its cycle? Reach for a crayon and draw the moon on your empty page. Tune in. Today might be a fast moon day for you, it might be a slow moon day; take as little or as long as you like with the colours and circle shapes as you draw the lunar body above. This is an initiatory, introductory process, a transitioning from the world of busy into your writing time. Decorate your moon if you desire or need; reflect as you do on the turning world around you; the rhythm of your world reflected in the swelling or fading moon. Use the crayons to spiral down onto the page, away from demands, beyond the control of others, away …

Exercise 2: Mind dump

Put the crayon down. Puuuuuut the crayon down – it's a thing, once a woman picks up a crayon she's often reluctant to lose it again. For the moment, put the crayon down and take a big, easy breath.

Pick up your pen. And dump what's on your mind onto the page, right here right now, in all its scramble, write whatever thoughts are traveling through your mind, just for a few minutes. Write. Whatever chatter is going on in there, let it run, let it loose, get it out of your mind and onto the page.

Immobilised? 'I don't know where to start' has a grip on your (probably throat) but for now pen will do. Or perhaps you feel resistance, a voice telling you 'this is stupid'? So write 'this is stupid'. Write 'I don't know where to start'. Write whatever words are spinning in your mind, write them. Over and over if needs be, write them. Your only task is to transcribe the words in your head onto the page.

It's scribble. So write it. Be the faithful scribe. Write whatever's there to write. It's blah. Just write! It's blah. It's dribble. Dump it. You don't ever have to look at it again. All that chatter. Move it on.

Set it free. Even if it's the same words over and over, *I don't know where to start I don't know where to start I don't know where to start this is driving me nuts I can't do this it's crazy it's crap it's stupid I'm over this and so on.*

What you write doesn't matter. What matters is you write. Just a few minutes. Off the top of your head. Phew. Glad we got that out of the way!

Exercise 3: The new learning

I know I said you wouldn't ever have to look at it again … whether or not you do is up to you. The invitation here is to either graze over what you've written, or feel into how you felt about facing the writing at all, and reflect:

What did I learn?
What did I learn about myself?
What did I learn about a situation?
What new information was revealed to me?

What did you learn? You may be horrified by so much nothing taking up space in your mind. It may be that you noticed a particular voice in your head you hadn't consciously realised was playing on a loop. It may be your awareness of your resistance to write, or speak, even to yourself …

What did you learn? Write it down.

Exercise 4: The Three Intelligences

Bring to mind a particular problem that is proving challenging at the moment – a difficulty, situation, encounter or individual, small or significant, it doesn't matter. Either way, if it's bothering you it's worth clearing from your field.

The First Intelligence: Mind

Now write. Write everything there is to know about this annoyance, problem or challenging situation or difficulty. Everything you know.

Start anywhere. Let your mind run, let it run riot, give yourself permission to say everything that needs to be said.

Who's in your story? What's the challenge? What's the problem? Who's the problem? What are they doing? What's so hard for you? What do you fear will happen? Away you go, the voices in your head, write write write write write. All of it. Onto the page.

As it is, onto the page. Reasonable and unreasonable, logical and illogical, infuriating and heartbreaking, onto the page. All of it. Uncensored. Beyond judgement. As it is. Onto the page.

Speak. Let your mind speak. Everything it has to say. Give yourself five minutes, ten minutes, whatever time you have, whatever time you need. Speak to yourself through the pen. You have permission now. You have all the room in the world. All the space you need to say everything bottled up inside you. Write it. Write it out.

Keep writing as I drop a few questions in now. They are prompts to call you onward. Doorways to deeper insight. By all means ignore them or ask your own questions. Keep writing as you consider:

Is there anything you can do to change the situation?

Or is the problem out of your control?

If it's out of your control, how do you feel about having no control?

Can you accept the problem, situation or challenge that's out of your control?

If so, what do you need to do to make peace with the situation, as it is?

Are you willing to do it? *No right no wrong, you don't have to do it. We're on a discovery mission, that's all.*

If you can change the situation, what action is required from you? *No right no wrong, you don't have to do anything, we're just shining a light.*

Are you willing to take that action? *No right no wrong, we're just telling ourselves what we know.*

If you are willing to take that action, what do you need to do?

What happens then? What do you need to prepare for?

What will change?

Are you sure? How do you know?

What do you fear? *No right no wrong, just telling ourselves the truth of the moment.*

Perhaps you know what you need to do but you are unwilling to take that action? *No right, no wrong.*

What will happen? Are you sure?

What do you fear will happen? What are you unwilling to risk? *No right no wrong. Just examining the lay of the land.*

What will happen? Do you know it will happen? *Are you sure?*

What else might happen?

Are you expecting other people to take action you're not willing to take? *No right no wrong. Just examining the lay of the land.*

Do you know it will happen? *Are you sure?*

What else might happen?

Do you think someone else should take action? *No right no wrong, no judgement. Tell the truth as you know it in this moment.*

Are you expecting others to do what you yourself are not willing to do? *No right no wrong, no judgement*

Do you think someone else should take action? *No right no wrong, no judgement. This is only between you and you. Write what you know, as best you know it.*

If you can't change the situation, what action might you take to lighten your relationship to it?

What else needs to be said?

Write. Write it out. Write it down.

The Second Intelligence: Body

Close your eyes. Take a deep breath. Breathe through the centre of your chest, breathing, through the heart. *The Writer's Breath.* Feet on the ground, breathing up from the Earth, all that energy. Spine straight. Sitting up. Feet on the ground. Spine flat if that's where you are. The energy of life riding your breath up from the Earth rising through your spine and out through the top of your head. Sky above. The wild spinning universe, all around you. Breathe. Through your skin. The air on your skin. Feel the air, the warmth of the sun, the cool of the night breeze. Life force. Rivers, mountains, wide flat plains. Life, all around you. Running through you. Life force, inside and outside. Breathing through your heart, come inside, welcome now, welcome, inside your skin. The bones, the flesh, the blood. The bones in your feet, your hands. Your ribs. On the inside. All your attention below the neck. Breathing. Inside your body. Aaahhh, yes. Breathing on the inside.

Return now to thinking about the problem or challenging situation you've been writing about.

Tune in closely. As you think about the problem, somewhere in your physical body there will be a response. A contraction. A pain. A niggle. Nausea. Tension. Tears. A twitch. Discomfort. It might be a rigid jaw. A headache. A queasy stomach. A tapping toe. Blinking eyes. A stiff neck. A sore throat.

Your body has a response to your story. Where? Where has the story landed in your body? Where has it taken root in your body?

Write it down.

Close your eyes again.

What is your body's story of the problem or challenge that is consuming you?

How does your body *feel* about what's on your mind?

Tune in. Physical responses are the language of the body. Emotions strike at your body, hence the word *feelings*. Let your body speak. Listen. Write. Your body has been sending you messages for a long time. Tune in. Pay attention now and write.

What does your body want you to know?

Write your body's story of what's on your mind. *No right no wrong, beyond judgement, we're listening now, not avoiding. We're telling ourselves the truth as we know it, that's all, just getting to know the lay of the land.*

Tune in to that part of your body – what does it need from you? *No right no wrong, you don't have to do anything, we're just gathering information.*

What does your body need from you?

Are you willing to give your body what it needs? *No right no wrong, no judgement.*

If yes, what do you need to do?

If not, why not? *No right no wrong, just know where you stand.*

If you give your body what it needs, what changes?

What changes if you are well?

What do you have to do if you are well that you do not have to do now?

What do you fear will be different if you are physically free from holding this story?

What will happen if you release your body from the burden of the problem? Are you still relevant to the lives of others involved in the situation? *No right no wrong, just telling the truth as best you know it. You don't have to do anything, just turning on the lights.*

Is there resistance in your body to the idea of freedom from this situation?

If so, where? Why? *No right no wrong.*

If your body could speak, what would it say to you? You are listening. This is your body's opportunity to speak to you … what does your body have to say? Write it down. All of it. Write it out.

The Third Intelligence: Heart

Breathing deeply. Through the centre. On the inside. Feet to the Earth. Breathing through the chest, inside your ribs. Breathing gently.

Now let your heart tell the story that's been troubling you.

What does your heart have to say about the problem or situation that is challenging you?

What does your heart know? What does it say to you?

Write it down. Be a faithful scribe, that's all that's asked from you now. You've come this far. What does your heart say?

It's a wrap.

Take a deep breath. Be still. You will have noticed distinctive differences between focusing your writing attention on those three places – mind, body, heart.

Yes? No? What did you notice? Write it down. What was the difference between those three sources of intelligence gathering?

For almost everyone there is a difference – but that doesn't mean to say there is for you. Some people express it like this: "It's as if the mind was full of the problem, while the heart knows exactly what to do."

And other people say this: "The mind was crammed with words, the heart's solution was simple."

And everyone says: "I know what I need to do."

We have the answer inside us. Always. It's in the body. We may not be able to control other people, and situations might be beyond our control. Regardless of what's going on around us we know what we need to do. We know. We know what we need to do. All that is left is whether or not we are up for the challenge of taking that action. All that's left is whether you're willing to do what you know needs to be done. The Three Intelligences will open you to the information you need and lead you to the crossroads of deliberate choice: problem or solution? If you know you are not ready to choose, or perhaps you know you will never choose, at least for now you are positioned to make peace in this place. For now.

Take that step and almost always what you know you need to do will lead you into unknown territory. This is deep breath country. Eventually, this practice will strengthen you. Grow you. Deliver you the courage you need to take the step that has taunted you for too long. Just one step. That's all that's asked from you. One step. One step in a new direction. One step and you're facing a new dawn. That one step will reveal the next step. That's what courage is. One step.

Exercise 5: Flick the switch

Now, for specific reasons, you're going to switch your focus.

This is a fast exercise: list three things you love in your life. Tell yourself why. Three things, 1 2 3.

List what you love and why?

What do you love? Why do you love it?

1 2 3.

Grab a crayon. Express what you love in colour and shape. It's not an art class. You're not being invited to create a masterpiece. Express your feelings through the crayons. That's all. Experiment with a different form of expression. There on the page, what you love in colour and random lines.

Why do this?

It's simple and it's worth remembering: journaling more often than not takes you into troubled waters, into the past. It is imperative that once you are done with each journey you return to the present. Here. Now. Where you are. Remembering what you love returns you to the moment that you're actually in with buoyancy and clarity.

Ready to begin, again.

Exercise 6: *That* person

Feet on the ground. Breathing.

Think of a person who annoys you. Who annoys you? Perhaps it is a small annoyance, perhaps it is someone you cannot bear. Who do you dislike, despise, loathe? If you have brought someone to mind who did you serious wrong, this exercise is challenging. You are the judge of whether or not you are ready for this challenge – if you are not, *no right no wrong no judgement,* move on to the next exercise. Return another day when you are stronger.

For those who are staying with us here: the person you have brought to mind, why do they annoy you? Why do you loathe them?

What gets to you about them? Write it down. Write it out. What annoys you, bothers you, seriously gets to you about x, y or z? Write it all out. If the person you bring to mind has done you serious wrong, and you are strong enough to explore this in writing, write out your thoughts and feelings, spill them onto the page.

And now.

What do you appreciate about this person? What do you appreciate about them and how is your life enhanced by their presence in your world?

Now this question may be easy or not easy, it may cause you sputter and curse, it may cause you distress. If you've come this far look deeper, stay with it, speak what you feel, think, believe, *know*.

For example: the same person who bugs you might also be a person of goodwill who mows your lawn. There are aspects of their personality that drive you nuts and other aspects you can appreciate. Find them. Name them. How are you shaped by this relationship? What does this relationship cultivate in you? Can you do better? Are you like them? How are you like them? What is asked from you to make peace with this person? What is asked from you to appreciate the whole of them?

Know yourself through your relationships.

If you brought to mind someone who did you serious wrong and you are meeting the challenge of this exercise, stay with the feelings, thoughts, emotions that rise, stay with them if you can. Know them. Yes, you know them well, you live with them. Are you ready to move them through? Perhaps not in one writing exercise, it might take several, that matters not. Go as far as you can and as far as you need. One step and put the pen down, if that's enough for you. If you've had enough and want done with the power of these emotions over you, let's ferry them to safety, above the high-water mark. Are you willing? Yes, of course you are. You've come this far. Let's take those one-steps towards setting you free.

The one who did you wrong, the one you never want to think about again, who is nonetheless running with the blood coursing through your beautiful body, that one: what have you learned as a result of your experience? Turn your focus there. What have you learned? What road do you need never take again as a result of this experience? What warning signs can you see flashing miles down the road that others do not see? What do you know that is ready to become a teaching for others? Your journey beyond, that is your task. There is teaching here in your experience with the one who wronged you. What personal power have you developed as a result of this experience? What strengths have you brought into the world that did not previously live in you or those around you? You are much, much more than your experience. Where are you victorious? Name these powers, strengths, victories. Name them. Know them.

Cultivate your strengths. Know yourself.

Exercise 7: You are what you see

Close your eyes. Breathing up from Earth.

Bring to mind a person you admire. It could be someone you know or someone you don't know, living or passed from our world – a family member, a friend, a shopkeeper, a celebrity, an activist, a spiritual master, even a book or movie character.

Who do you admire and why? Write it out.

Now the kicker. Close your eyes. Take a gentle breath on the inside.

This one's a question for your heart.

The person you admire: how are you like them? Write it down. How are you like the person you admire? Write.

This is not an easy exercise. The discomfort it can cause is increased plentifold when people in workshops are witnessed sharing who they admire and how they are like this person. It is commonplace for people to cringe and splutter and find small attributes for how they are like the person they admire, for example: "Well we both have brown hair." They die a thousand deaths as they are tricked into recognising the pure science of the moment, the universal law of reflection: we are what we see. What you admire in others is the best of you. That person may have cultivated and refined those aspects and put them to work on a bigger stage. That doesn't change the fact you are like them.

You are what you see. They are showing you the best of you. They are your guiding light. They are a little further along the road, to be sure; they are lighting your way.

Strange isn't it? How we are so ready to speak the best in others, reluctant to acknowledge the best of ourselves.

Those words you wrote about the person you admire: *this is who you are.*

Close your eyes again. Bring to mind the problem, situation or challenge you were writing about when you were writing The Three Intelligences, mind, body and heart.

The person you admire – what would s/he say to you about this challenge? Write it down. What would the person you admire advise you?

Exercise 8: The miracle of you

What are you looking forward to tomorrow? Simple really. Write it down.

What are you looking forward to tomorrow? Reach for a crayon, express your anticipation in colour and squiggles.

A simple exercise to close, yes. Simple and straightforward. What are you looking forward to tomorrow?

Write. However many words are there to write, one or three or a hundred. Write what you are looking forward to tomorrow.

It's been said before and it's worth repeating: journaling will almost always take you into the past and often return you to difficult situations, primarily because the situations that hurt us are the ones we hold onto, the ones that live on in our hearts and bodies, the ones we have yet to transform into wisdom and absorb into our way of being.

Always finish your journaling by returning to the present, re-entering your life, work, family, community with positive-as-you-can thoughts transmitting from your mind, body and heart. This is not to suggest you have to pretend in your everyday life, to fake happy, to gush delight. It is to suggest there's a time and a place for past emotions that have been deliberately summoned and it is in your interests to cultivate their management. The whole point of journaling is not just to make peace, it is to *be* peace. It is a life's work, to be sure.

Try this: close your eyes. Just for a blink or three.

Think of something fabulous that you love, think of what you love.

Now think of something that's bothering you, something that you loathe.

Do you notice a difference in the way each of these thoughts feels in your body?

Can you feel the power that is available to you? In any moment.

You have the power to decide how you feel. The power to decide how your story goes. The power to determine, at any time, how you meet the moment. That doesn't mean you pretend to be happy. That doesn't mean it's easy to decide how you feel. It does mean, with practice, you can choose the energy with which to meet the world around you in ways that don't undermine the integrity of your being, in some or many or even most situations, depending on your relationship to the story.

Writing negatives releases them from your body. Writing positives will make you feel lighter, stronger, better able to meet challenges. Make a habit of journaling. Let it clear your being: mindbodyspirit.

Write the downside until you're empty. And always finish your journaling with a positive. Leave the emotions that have surfaced where they belong, in the past and on the page!

Journaling will make space for new ideas, new emotions, new thoughts.

It's your story, you are learning to tell it the way you like.

12-2 EVERY BODY'S STORY
Your life, your health, your story

YOUR BODY holds your life story. It's right there in how you stand, how you sit, how you walk. Every story you've ever told lives inside your body, for better or for worse, in sickness and in health. Your ability to run, or bend easily. Stiff joints, inflexible muscles, shallow breathing … there they are, the sharp inhale of moments lived and not forgotten, events you've loved or loathed, series of circumstances you'd rather forget, there they are. Stories long past, living now, inside your body.

Your thoughts and attitudes – summed up in the stories you tell about yourself and others – are shaping and even creating your health and your disease, your sanity and your destabilised emotional states. *You are not powerless.* Your responses to life, aka the stories you tell, are having the time of their life inside your body, running riot through the house, taking up residence in your blood, your bones, your flesh.

There's a high likelihood you're not paying attention to your invited guests.

Here's a fact that is likely to do your head in: the body has no independent will. No thoughts. No ideas. No emotions. It is a flesh and blood entity that has biological intelligence. That's it. The rest – all story. All those affections and afflictions that run through you, the wonderful times flooding your system with the invincible force of life when it is going your way; the hard times, bringing you down (literally), etched into your bones. Physical responses to thoughts and emotions. Your emotional responses determine whether your interior guests are toxic or tame. *Sick to the stomach, rigid joints, terrorised tissue, depressed spirits.*

Stories. All stories. Your stories.

It's your story, you decide how it goes.

Collective stories

A panic has taken hold in the west and its story has three faces. The panic is colonising our bodies. It's having its wicked way with us. Burrowing in to our being. Destabilising our health and wellbeing.

The first face: the 'safe' story

Not so long ago we waved people out the door with 'have a great time'. Now we farewell them with 'travel safe'. And we don't have to be going very far to have this depressing chorus trailing after us – 'be safe' we appeal to our children as we drop them at school; 'be safe' we petition adults heading off to work; 'I love you' we call after them, fortifying our fears just in case it's the last time we ever see them, transmitting our fears to children who are learning to confuse panic with love.

Leaving aside the reality that in the west humans have never been 'safer', just how exactly are we to 'be safe'? What's the alternative? And what does that mean – 'be safe'? If 'something happens' did I fail the safety test? Should I have not … what … got on a particular bus, driven down a particular road at a particular time, stopped for a drink with friends, stayed home, walked out the door … what?! See? Crazy making.

Know your fears. Choose the reality of 'what is' over 'what if'.

Write your way to solid ground.

The second face: the 'sorry' story

Sorry. Sorry sorry sorry sorry sorry sorry. How sorry is a human being supposed to be in a day? Seriously! This is a crazy turn of linguistic and emotional events. Crazy. Stop it. Stop. And pay attention.

Sorry. Sorry for what?

Our sorries are meaningless awful. *Meaningless*. Awful. It is as if we are apologising for living. Apologising for breathing. Apologising for existing in the same space as another. We now have children whose every second word is 'sorry'.

Save 'sorry' for the those moments we have truly, deeply, personally or collectively erred, when we have done wrong by another and we are courageous enough to dig deep, take a solid breath, look the one we have wronged in the eye and say: 'I'm sorry.' The rest of it, blah, say hello instead. Grin at the synchronicity of your timing as you both step this way and that in your attempt to move past the one in your way. Hello! Share a chuckle. Save your sorries.

The third face: the 'busy' story

Busy. Too-busy. So-busy. And my personal favourite: crazy-busy. And yes we are. Crazy-busy 'achieving' our 'goals' and visionboarding our 'success' and plotting our children's 'future'. Hooray for us.

While collectively we live out the manic terrors of safe and sorry. Our responses to the sorry busy safe world we have created around us are taking up residence inside us. Our health systems are buckling under the pressure. Mental health is a growth industry. Cancer is a growth industry. Security is a growth industry. Panic is a growth industry. Isn't it ironic then that 'wellbeing' is also a growth industry?

Wellness fuelled by fear is not wellness. Health driven by obsession is not health. Sanity shaped by the sharp stab of an unreleased inhale is not sanity. All this going on inside your living body. Your living body, shaped by story. It's your story, you decide how it goes. Your story is the one thing, the only thing, over which you actually do have control. A super-power, if you like.

Every Body's Story is your personalised safe sorry crazy-busy don't-make-yourself-sick time-out zone.

So come now, come inside.

There's no place like home

Something happens 'to' us. We tell a story about it. We load it with emotion. We tell ourselves there is something to fear. We amplify the story by uploading it into our body. We transmit the story. And our health expands or contracts accordingly.

This is the power of story.

S/he/they did (…) *to* me. And perhaps they did. The only time this is possibly true is in the moment 'they' did it. After that, well after that the truth of the moment, aka the rest of your life, depends on the story you tell. The phantoms you let into the house. The spooks who take up residence because you're not home to keep the cobwebs clear. *This is not to suggest you deny the impacts of events on you; nor is it to suggest there is only one way to tell the story and that the story must be 'positive'.* It is to suggest that stories are traveling instruments; they change as we move through life. Your identification with a story can become a role you play, a mask you wear, a way of getting what you want, a way of denying yourself and others the truth of your existence, a way of staying small, playing small … until it becomes too much to bear and you explode or implode, taking your body down with you.

Your task is to tell the truth as you know it this passing moment, to tell this truth in the privacy of your own heart.

Tell yourself your passing truth and watch how your language frames your story. Rather than giving power to others in your story, i.e., 'they did (…) to me', try '(…) happened'.

After that, there is the story you tell (your business) and the story others impose upon you (not your business). Wellness demands you do not become your story. Others, perhaps in need of a victim, perhaps in need of a symbol, perhaps in need of an enemy, will attempt to hijack your story, to frame it for you, to offer you an easy out. *The poisoned apple at Snow White's door.* Will you surrender your sovereignty? *Sleep for a hundred years?* There is no free ride here. *No pop culture Prince*

Charming to save you. Will you take responsibility or give others carte blanche in your home? *Mirror, mirror on the wall.* It's your story. You decide how it goes.

It takes courage to take up residence on the inside of your body. It would be a mistake to underestimate the discipline it takes to live there, on a permanent basis. *Every Body's Story* will give you real time experience of just how much time you spend on the inside. *Anywhere but here.*

Living on the inside is also known as 'presence'. People who occupy their skin are confident, sure-footed. They are alert to what's going on around them. They have eyes that see and ears that hear. They are less likely to misread situations. They know how others receive and perceive them, and whether or not to take things personally (usually not). They know their story and are alert to what is 'real' (very little). The body is a transmission device, sending and receiving. When you take up residence on the inside you are in charge of the transmitter; if you have just moved in you are positioned to learn the controls.

I knew a woman who lost her lover to another woman. The emotional legacy of this event embarrassed and defined her. Years later, she had the opportunity to win her lover back. She took it. Her lover moved in. And that weekend the woman broke her leg on the soccer field, wrapped it around the stocky shin of a mid-fielder hell-bent on preventing her from shooting that goal. I was there on the field with her. From the ground, before the pain of her shattered shin washed over her, she looked up at me and said: "I know why I did this. I had to win." She wasn't speaking of the ball.

I spoke to her soon afterwards, when she was home, thigh deep in plaster. I asked her what she meant, *I had to win*. She said it was the first time in her life she had played sport with no awareness of what else was going on around her. She was driven to shoot that goal with a fury that broke her. She wanted to win. So too the lover she was done with, now returned to her life. She had wanted to win.

The woman took responsibility for what happened to her on the field. She spent no energy blaming the mid-fielder for a collision that cost her three months in plaster. She blamed no-one. It was she who was rigid, angry, tight with the self-destructive knowing she had made a terrible mistake (cajoling her lover to return to her life); she who had been unwilling to face up to its remedy (the lover had to go). She knew she was responsible for the extreme reality that now bit hard in her life. She knew what she needed to do and it is too easy to say 'she let her lover go'. The reality was the lover had given up an entire life to move north to be with her. Everything. Work. House. Relationship. All because my friend had to win. *Shame.* Redress for rejection. *Exile.* And now she must face her role in the shattering that was about to occur in the life of another. *Self-forgiveness.* Face up. Eyes straight. Take responsibility. Tell the truth. The price of peace in the human heart/h.

Every Body's Story

Come inside. Come in before you go out. Occupy your skin. Know what is shaping and driving your inner world. Pay attention to the voices in your head. Tell yourself the passing truth. Learn to live on the inside of your skin, yes, here on the inside. Instead of abandoning your body to your personalised story of shame and self-loathing, take up residence. Live your life from the inside, beyond safe and sorry and the kind of busy that makes us crazy-sick. Challenge the grip old stories have on your body, your life. Move the old stories on. Learn how to prevent new stories from landing.

Come, let's take a good look at the stories we hold in our joints, tissue, energy fields. Let's clean the house so we might take up residence. Let's write our way home.

For *Every Body's Story* you will need room to move. Stretch out. A yoga mat if you have one. Floor space at the very least. Even rocky ground will do if the privacy you seek takes you beyond domestic dwelling. If you are wheelchair bound or bedbound, you have capacity for this exercise.

Grab your notebook and pen.

The writing exercises that follow are an introduction to the concept that your body holds your story. The more you practise these writing exercises, the more deeply you will understand your body. You will learn to master the grip old stories have on your life and your health. The exercises that follow are a journey, an exploration, an expedition into the shadows of your internal house.

It is a lifetime's work. We may as well begin.

Clearing a path to the front door

Sitting on your mat, on the floor, on the rocky earth, on a chair if you can't make it to the floor.

Off the top of your head, write. Do a mind dump. All that chatter, download it onto the page. Blah. Whatever's occupying space in your head today. Move it on. Move it out. Faithful scribe. Write the random. Clear the debris. Dump it onto the page. Five minutes, phew.

Preparing to enter

You've cleared the debris along the path to your house. You stand at the front door. You need the key.

So reach for it.

If you have a yoga practice do a few rounds of *Surya Namaskar*, the sun salutations.

If you have an exercise regime, go through a specific mat routine that takes you from standing to lying flat, returning to standing (about ten minutes).

If you have no particular practice, do what you can of the following, take it easy, don't force it – if you do not have balance enough to stand, do as much as you can in your chair or other resting device:

- stand up straight

- stretch your arms above your head, hold them there
- bend forward and hang there for a few breaths
- roll your spine up to standing straight again
- stretch your arms out sidewards, hold them there
- bend forward
- come to the floor, kneeling on all fours
- come to plank, or push-up position
- kneel on all fours
- still kneeling, push your bottom back towards your feet and lay your body over your knees, head on the floor, arms relaxed in front or beside your body (also known as child pose)
- kneel on all fours
- sit cross-legged
- lie down on your back
- pull your knees to your chest
- raise your legs and point your toes to the ceiling
- lower your legs
- roll over onto your belly
- kneel
- stand.

Be still. Stand still. Feet together. Stand straight. Look ahead. Breathe through your nose. Keep breathing. Stay there, don't move.

Rest.

It doesn't matter how you move or how much, what matters is that you move, in whatever way you can in the confines of the space you're in, with consideration for your current physical abilities. Move. Breathe.

Yoohoo, anybody home?

Breathe. The key to the door of your house is your breath. Take a deep one. You'll need it. We're through the door. It's dark inside. Who's in the house? Is anybody home? It's time to investigate. Come, come on in, come on through.

Come to the floor or as close to the ground as you can. Get comfortable, as best you can. Rest for a moment, get a feel for the place while your eyes get used to the dark. Blink into the shadows. Close your eyes. Breathe.

The Writer's Breath. Breathing deeply, breathing gently, breathing sweetly. On the inside of your skin. On the inside with the bones and the blood and the flesh. Yes, here. Get a feel for the place. While your eyes adjust to the light.

The comfort zone

In the sequence of movements you've just experienced there will be one position that put you totally at ease. One position or pose that is right inside your comfort zone. A way of resting in your house that makes it yours, a way of holding your body that causes no discomfort, no distress, no rising panic. It might be a resting place, a hiding place or a place of power. It is the position you don't want to leave.

Find that position now. Go there. Get to know your body as it finds this place. Be in it. Feel it. Hold it.

Write it. Fold yourself to the mat or chair and write what it is you love about this position. Write out how it feels. What are your emotional responses to this position? Describe them. Are there stories attached to holding this position? What is asked from you here? What are you free from here? Why does it feel safe?

Return to the pose. Feel it again. Know it more deeply. You are gathering intelligence. What else is here for you? What more is there to know? About yourself? About your relationship to your body? About the stories you hold here?

Feel it. Hold it. Describe it. Write it. Test it. Explore it further.

What is it about this position that is so deliciously comfortable for you?

It's okay in here

Of all the movements you've just practised there will be one that is 'okay'. Doable but by no means great. A pose or position you can hold easily enough with a little effort. A place in your house you can put up with; no need to renovate, no need to cause a fuss.

As with the exercise above, find that pose now. It may mean going through your routine again, watching for 'it's okay'.

Find the position (there's highly likely to be more than one; find the one you want to work with today). Get to know your body as it seeks out this place. Find the position. Be it. Feel it. Hold it.

Write it. Fold yourself to the mat or chair as you explore writing your responses to this position. How does it feel? What are your emotional responses to this position? Describe them. Are there stories attached to finding this position? Are there stories attached to holding this position? What is asked from you here? What in this pose is not wonderful? What minor discomfort do you need to overcome? Is there a story here?

Return to the pose. Feel it again. How are you breathing here? Know the position more deeply. You are gathering intelligence. What else is here for you? What more is there to know? About yourself? About your relationship to your body? About the stories you hold here?

Feel it. Hold it. Describe it. Write it. Test it. Explore it further.

Run for your life!

The routine you practised will contain at least one position you loathed. A pose you couldn't leave fast enough. A posture best avoided at all costs, or perhaps the terror lay in getting into or out of that posture.

If you have a regular yoga or exercise practice, you may need to pull from the entire theatre of postures available to you for this exercise. You are casting about for a pose that is a struggle for you, not necessarily the one that is a challenge due only to your lack of mastery. You are looking for the one you resist. The one you avoid. A way of holding your body that causes your breathing to run fast and shallow, where holding the pose makes you want to run for your life.

You don't want to go there. You don't want to be there. You can't get out of the house fast enough. *Anywhere but here.*

As with the above exercises, find that pose now. It may mean going through your routine again, watching for the place best avoided.

Find the position. Get to know your body as it seeks out this place. Find the position. Be it. Feel it. Hold it. Breathe. Breathe! There is an intruder in the house. Breathe. Adjust your eyes to the light. Listen. Watch.

Write it. Be comfortable on the mat as you explore in writing your responses to holding this posture. How do you feel? What are your emotional reactions to this position? Describe them. Are there stories attached to finding this position? Are there stories attached to holding this position? What is asked from you here? Why the need to run? Why the tears? Why the sharp inhale? What terror do you need to overcome? What is the story here? Who is in the house with you? Who else is here?

Return to the pose. Feel it again. How are you breathing here? Know the position more deeply. You are gathering intelligence. What else is here for you? What more is there to know? About yourself? About your relationship to your body? About the stories you hold here?

Feel it. Hold it. Describe it. Write it. Test it. Explore it further.

Make peace in this place. Breathe. Relax with each breath. Surrender the stories you hold in your joints and muscle tissue. Cry softly if you must, howl if it suits you. Release the hold this story has on your life. It might take five minutes, it might take five days or five years. Revisit this place until it holds no more power over you.

#courage

Home truths

Take a break. Have a drink of water. Lay down on your mat. Rest. Close your eyes, or graze the ceiling with your eyes gently open, whatever works for you. What matters is you rest. Take a break from your story. Time out. A moment. Breathe easy. Rest.

In *Embodied Journaling* you were introduced to The Three Intelligences. We're going to call on them now.

Sitting up. Comfortable now. Notebook within easy reach. Close your eyes and breathe *The Writer's Breath*. Breathing through the centre of your chest. Breathing the lifeforce all around you, through your skin. Breathing. On the inside with the bones and the blood and the flesh. Breathing.

Bring to mind one insight you've had today. About a problem. About a significant health or body issue. About a person of influence shaping your response to this problem or issue. About a story living inside you. About resistance or some other dynamic force inhabiting your body.

Choose one insight. Write all your mind knows about your insight onto the page. Empty your mind. All you know about your issue, problem or incapacity. Pour it out. The stories, the myths, the excuses. The people in this story. All of it. Tell yourself the truth. What did you find, spill it onto the page.

Close your eyes. Feel the insight in your body. Feel the connection to the problem or health issue or incapacity. Where is it? Where does it live? How does it feel? How does your body hold this story? What does your body need you to know?

What does your body need from you? Are you willing to give this to your body? Yes or no, *no right no wrong, no judgement*. A simple question: are you willing to give your body what it needs for relief from this story? If not, why not? You may have very good reasons for holding onto this pain or discomfort. Even so, what price are you willing you pay for it? Why? What price do you fear you will pay? If you are willing to give your body what it needs, what is your first step? What do you need to do to relieve your body of the burden of this story?

Questions now via The Three Intelligences of mind, body and heart.

Dance the questions around and through your being, let the answers come. Write. Write them out.

How does this health issue define your life?

How does this limitation benefit you? *Serious question, no right no wrong.*

How does it benefit or interfere with the lives of others?

How does it interfere with your life? Your needs?

What are you able to avoid due to this problem or health issue? Where are you off the hook? *No judgement, just mapping the terrain.*

What responsibilities are you relieved of because you can't …? *No right no wrong, just getting the lay of the land.*

What are you owed because of your issue or incapacity?

Who owes you?

Who are you without this incapacity? Who are you?

What would you have to do, for yourself or others, if you did not have this issue, reason, excuse or justification?

Who else is in your story?

Does this person hold you to ransom? A voice in your head? *Tell the passing truth of this moment.*

Or perhaps this person is beholden to you courtesy of your issue or incapacity? *No right no wrong.*

Either way, are you willing to let them go? *No right no wrong, just shining light on the shadows.*

What is required from you to let this person go?

What happens then? *Feel this space.*

Who are you if your body is free from the forces of others?

Write. Write it out. Hear your body's story. Empty your body and mind of the burden of this load. Tell yourself the truth. Write.

The one you admire

In *Embodied Journaling* we explored the best of ourselves through the person we admire.

Call on that person now.

What would the person you admire have to say to you about the situation you've been writing about? What would s/he say?

Write it down.

Other people's houses

Give thought to the dreadful burdens we place on others when we tell stories about them. Watch. You'll be surprised how often you have something to say about other people. Come home. Your business is here. Your business has no business telling stories about others. You will pay a price. And it won't be pretty. Watch, the next time you tell a story about another, watch for the emotion you upload into your body. Where does it land? What's the impact on your health? Ask yourself: what is my need to tell this story? What's in it for me? *Tell the truth.* How do I feel when I tell this story? Do I need others to share this story too? What do I need the other person to feel? *Shame?* Am I safer or stronger if I can compel others to collude with my story? *Exile?* Am I shoring up my own terror through by shaming another? *Self-forgiveness?*

Telling stories about others. *Not your business.*

Home is where the heart/h is

The safe sorry busy stressors, blah, not worth the price, not worth the space, be done with them. Take responsibility, full responsibility, for everything you perceive, everything you do, everything you say, think, feel. This is not to say 'be perfect' and it is not to say everything's your fault and it is not to say your life is without influence in your world (cultural, political, economic, familial – very little is in reality a 'choice'). It is to say 'take responsibility' for recognising your responses to life. And understand it's okay to hurt in this place. 'Take responsibility' is not an admonition. It's not a summons to rigidity. Responsibility is the alternative to collapse. It's the only thing you can actually do. You cannot control what others do. You can absolutely control how you tell the story. It's called maturity.

It's your house. Your hearth. Show up. Surrender powerlessness.

I didn't say it was easy. When your story is prefaced with 'he', 'she' and 'they', odds on you are vacating your premises. *He did me wrong. She is such an x. They are y.* Instead of going to war, or falling apart, *see the language there?*, take a breath, show up for yourself, listen to your body and use the information available to you. *I am vulnerable here.* What action do you need to take on your own behalf that strengthens you? *I am expecting others to do what I am unwilling to do for myself: save me.* She may have done x. Maybe he is y. Perhaps they are z. Or maybe it wasn't about you at all. The more you get real and the more responsibility you learn you can take, the greater the understanding will be that nothing is personal. Regardless of what he, she, they did or do, it's not about you. *What do I represent to this person?* They have the power to destabilise your sense of wellbeing only if you are vulnerable to attack in this place. *What action must I take on my own behalf?*

Are you expecting others to give you want you are not willing to give yourself? Are you outsourcing your dis-ease? Before you run for the nearest doctor find the story. *Is it real?* Meet the challenges of shame (*root it out*), exile (*no fear*) and self-forgiveness (*come home, where you belong*). Prevent new stories from moving in, settling in among your bones and your flesh and your vital organs. Okay, so it's hard … really? Harder to be well than unwell? Actually, yes, *yes it is*.

Recover your willingness to be well. Move your body, every day move, every day be still, every day rest. Keep your life force flowing. Breathe. Reach for the passing truth of the moment. Be still. Breathe deeply. Breathe slowly. Come home. Come in to go out. Unwilling to abandon the house any longer. Surrender the agony of bearing the untold story inside you.

Knit your soul to the inside of your skin.

Make peace with your heart/h.

12-3 THE STORY OF YOUR HEART
Following Ariadne's thread

IN MOROCCO, there is a tradition of oral storytelling called *hikayat*. Master storytellers and their apprentices, weaving tall tales and true in public squares amidst the cooking fires, spice sellers and snake charmers. In Morocco, they say that to know the truth of your existence you must first know the story of your heart. This story is Ariadne's thread, leading us into the labyrinth, guiding us out again.

The story of your heart is the story of your life. Not the one you tell, the one outside your world of words. Beyond thought. A long way from identity. The self behind self. The treasure long buried. The whisper within.

You are the only one who knows this story.

Not the Story of Your Heart

Meeting the story of your heart requires you to go gently into the land of far beyond. It is a privileged place. A place of honour. It asks much from you. Before you set out, there are loose ends to tie. Resentment is a loose end. So too entitlement. Not shame, no. Shame is where you retreated from the story of your heart. Justification, loose end.

We'll make this swift, though the answers may take some time. Revisit often. Got your pen? Scrap paper will do.

Three short questions

Feet on the ground. Close your eyes. Writer's Breath. Write at least fifteen minutes on each question. If you are angry, spill it now. If you are resentful, now is your time. If you are sulking, dump it here.

What do you want that's a waste of your time?
What do you want because others have it?
How have you been robbed?

The Story of Your Heart

The story of your heart asks nothing more from you than you know it. That's it. This is the place of peace. The price of peace. Yours, to have and to hold.

Meeting the story of your heart is a night journey. It requires a willingness to go gently into the darkness. To enter the encounter softly. Kindly. To come in peace.

To meet the story of your heart, make preparations. The kind of effort you might make for a lover. Candles. Music. Cushions. Comfort. A long bath. A delicate feast. Wine in a beautiful glass. A small fire for warmth and soft lighting. A blank notebook, beautiful, sacred.

Prepare for the evening. Settle in. Raise your glass, toast the journey ahead. Rest. Close your eyes. Breathe gently. And travel in. Your body not thinking, breathing. Travel softly and meet your beloved.

Silent

Silence. That which you will not speak. The voice denied. The one in retreat. Choked. Shamed. Fearing exile.

We tell ourselves the story we can live with, the story we can bear. We tell others the story we can live with, the story we believe will bear scrutiny under the sharp gaze of their merciless judgement.

Now we seek the voice that was silenced.

Each of these short phrases is an exercise. Gently now, tuning in to the softness and sweetness around you, the music, the cushions, the fire. Close your eyes and meet your silence.

Listen, the whisper within.

What is it you cannot speak?

Write. Write gently. Pour your soft words onto the page.

The words from the beloved within. Her words. Not the sharp, interfering wordbarbs of others. They have said enough. Not the story others tell. Her story. Only her.

Meet your silence. Wrap a shawl around her. Listen to her. Hear her story. She is relying on you to remember. You are her witness and her scribe. Listen as she pours out her story, and write.

Broken

Aaaah, the broken hearted. You are not alone on this island. This is the human condition. Our hearts break. We tell stories to mask, mend, hide, recoil. And yet the broken heart is our greatest source of strength. Run as we feel we must as far from this place as possible … keep running by all and every means … seeking, seeking, seeking the safe place beyond … *anywhere but here.*

You cannot outrun the broken heart. The broken heart is your safe place. It is the truth of you. It is time to return. Not ready for the journey? Feel this moment. Meet it. Go as far as you bravely can at this time. By all means turn back. Follow the thread back through the silence, return the way you came. The thread is here, to follow again another night. The story of your heart is beyond. Waiting for you. It will wait for you. As long as it takes. Your beloved, waiting for you.

If you are journeying on …

Here we meet the broken heart. The broken breaking shattered heart. Our point of greatest power. It is here we find our kindness. Our compassion. Here is our sadness and our willingness to rise again. Here we meet what was loved. What was lost. Here is our self-forgiveness, as we meet the slow dawning realisation that no one did anything to us. And face the horror that our riot of rage and resentment was an attack on ourself. An outsourcing of responsibility to another or others. Oh my breaking heart. My sorrow.

My wasted time. You broke and I was not there for you. I broke and sought solace from others who failed me, failed me, failed me. I see now they failed me because there was nothing they could do, it was I who failed to stand solid for me, I who felt shamed and loathed and shattered. I who thought I did not exist without the conditional reflection of another … And yet all that was asked from me was that I stay here, stay, stay with the broken heart. Stay true. Hold the centre. Be here. Never leave.

I am here now.

Write the story of your broken heart. Not the she did, he did, this happened, that happened, he said, she said version of your story, for that is the stories of others. Not the wounded, bitter, probably self-righteous 'I' story either.

Shhhh, there's another story within. The story of your broken heart. Whole and true.

Write. Follow the thread through the quiet darkness and write the story of your broken heart. Write the journey home. Write the return. Write the recovery. Write the beauty of this place now wild and no longer forlorn.

Whole

Stoke your fire. Sip your wine. Sup from the feast you have prepared. Ready now for the final stage of your journey through the labyrinth and into the centre.

You are writing the story of your heart. And that's all there is to it. There are no things in this story, no people, no identities, no I wants and no I shoulds.

There is only the story of your heart.

What matters to your heart? The sacred one, now witnessed. Behind the cascading curtain of voices within and beyond the reach of right and wrong, the story of your heart. It's there in love and longing. Far away words that offer you all there is to know in this moment. Reach for them, reach for them now, let them know you're here. Settle back and wait, let them come. Close your eyes. They are here. They are here. Waiting for you. Ready to embrace you, hold you, celebrate and welcome you.

The story of your heart. Your sacred heart. Write. Write the story of your heart.

And now live, from here.

12-4 THE HAUNTING
Stalking the shadows

EVERY HUMAN life, no matter how well-loved and lived, has its shadows. The shifting shapes that lurk just outside our vision. Mercurial ghosts that tip over chairs just when we've arranged things nicely. Wraiths that call at the strangest hour, a whisper on the breeze to *pay attention*, a rap on the door urging you to run like hell. Like spots on the sun, stare straight at them and they slip sideways. Blink and they're gone.

I knew a woman who could not allow herself luxuries without finding someone of disadvantage to bring along with her. For all the reasons she could summon to explain her noble compulsions, generosity and self-sacrifice among them, underpinning her philanthropic reasoning lay a deep sense of self-denial. She was not worthy of her privilege, despite having worked hard for it. Her husband was in the shadows (she was spending 'his' money). Her father too (putting his daughter in her place).

The woman too clever. The spirit too bright. The personality too bold. She had sought shelter in 'goodness' (though her wild wolf tail was always visible beneath her skirts). At 70 she broke her heart. Literally. She broke her heart and ended up on the surgeon's table. And with recovery after the breaking came the turning tide that carried her away and washed her up on a distant shoreline, ready to claim the life that was awaiting her beyond the sacrifice she had misnamed 'service' to others; facing now the vacuum of terror that is the slow dawning realisation that those to whom she had devoted her life could not care less about the actuality of her; that their story of her had and has nothing to do with who she is, or was; that they have no interest in understanding the too-late-to-turn-back journey she has embarked upon that will deliver to her the woman she is tomorrow.

There are many shadows in this story. They are not real. They do not exist. Every single one of them lives only in the woman's imagination. Her father is long dead. So too her husband. Yet they live on in the haunted house of the untended garden of the human mind. They shape her identity, her actions, her living relationships. Such power ... *they broke her heart.*

We bequeath them too much credit.

Scratch the surface of the dark. Let in the light and we will find more than the husband and the father. Who else is lurking in the shadows? Let's call them daemons, lesser divinities of mythic Greek origin that shape who we are and have no bias towards 'good' or 'evil'. Cast out one daemon and you will find another, and another, and another. Always another ghost to stand between, or compel you towards, human longing and the impulse to act on our own behalf. Always another wraith to excuse you from acting for yourself. *Courage.* What role does this woman need her daemons to play for her? *Everything starts with a thought.* The woman was exhausted from the serial untruths she had been telling herself for years, decades. She had buckled, not beneath the burden of the ghosts lurking in the shadows, but the story-lies she had told about them. Through her justifications and excuses about them and for them, about and for herself, she had too long ignored – feared, snubbed – the haunting shadows. She had refused and face-on failed to endure the glare of shame and self-loathing reflected in the darkness. *Full responsibility.* A physical burden that became too much to bear, *oh my breaking heart.*

The woman has a big bark. A guard dog tethered to the gateway of her philanthropic heart. She terrifies the timid and enrages the self-important. The bark is the gatekeeper of bewildering grief. The unwilling and the unkind and the self-righteous say she is 'too outspoken'. And we might say: they censor her, where those who are less than strong would be silenced. Only we won't say this. We will say: she censored herself in response to the criticisms of those around her. We will say: people readily silence themselves fearing the harshness of others.

We know now others do nothing to us, although of course they do; they do, they do. And we comply with their assault: our survival, our price of belonging, our reflection in the ones we love and, likely, to whom we have given far too much. You might say, as others before you have said: "but it's hard."

Yes. Yes, it is hard. It is hard hard hard. Yet full responsibility for the feeling body that does your living – which paradoxically is forever entangled and entwined with others – is the path that will return power to your hands, restore strength to your heart, and clarity to your mind. It is hard. And we endure, the panic attacks, the breathlessness, the sudden tears. They keep hurting us. Yes they do. They keep hurting us. Yes they do. And because they are family or others our televised world defines as 'loved ones' we keep showing up. And showing up. And showing up.

It is hard. Responsibility is hard. And it's our task to make it soft. And the cold stone fact of the matter is if you are haunted by your past you will be afraid of your future. There is no point delaying the journey any longer. As that legendary archetypal cowboy John Wayne said, courage is being scared to death and saddling up anyway.

The Haunting

What haunts you? Who lurks in the shadows of your mind? How are you crippled, shamed, limited by that which you wilfully do not see? What do you turn away from in others? In yourself?

Curious? Terrified? Perhaps both?

Grab your notebook and pen. A cup of tea. A glass of wine. A water bottle. Find your resting place. Get comfortable. And breathe. Come to Earth. Feet on the ground. Close your eyes. Breathe through your centre, through your heart. All of life transmitting around you, call it in. Breathe life through your skin. Call it in. Come inside with your bones and your blood and your flesh. Inside.

As always, the questions below are portals, entryways into the journey that is yours to explore. Descend and return. That is the law. You can visit the underworld. You cannot stay. That is the law.

Three writing exercises follow: The one word, Beads of shelter, The gatekeeper. Each exercise unfurls a list of questions. You are not required to answer all the questions. Though if you have come this far you are required to start. From the top. Write your way through them. You will know which questions are for you, which ones you absolutely must tend. You will know, for you will react. You will resist. Resistance accompanied by a flash flood of internal verbiage is your signal to pay attention. Equally, pay attention to those questions you dismiss as 'too simple'. Stalk your responses, they are your clue to the 'magic spot' that will turn the wall and admit you entry to the inner world of your feeling body. When you have no story at all about a question you may be reasonably satisfied you are free of that particular entangled rope.

Adapt the questions. Follow their threads. Let the haunting shadows lead you to the truth of your heart, your world. Like the story monsters of childhood, ultimately they will lead you home.

The one word

There is a word others use to describe you. Your family of origin word might be quite different to your work-world word, which might be different again from your social world word or even the gym world word. It's worth noting that positive words can be as crippling to your self-identity as negative words: good greedy selfish shy angry strong nice good aggressive miserable happy bossy martyr good nasty independent … what's the word that echoes in your ears? The word will often and easily be prefaced by 'too'. You are too … what?

The family word ...

Let's start with family, by which we mean the human beings amongst whom you spent your childhood.

Close your eyes. Breathe gently on the inside, from the centre.

The word. You have heard it often. You can hear it now.

What is the family word for you? Write the word.

The work-world word ...

What's the one word colleagues might use to describe you? Perhaps it is the same word? Perhaps a different word. Close your eyes. Hear the word. Write the word.

The social world word

How do friends and acquaintances describe you?

What's their one word? Write the word.

There are now three words on your page. Look at them. Bold on blank paper. The words others use to describe you. Feel them. They are reverberating through your body, your identity. Breathe. Come home. Stay here, inside your skin. Cry if you must. Breathe.

Now roll through the questions below and write as you go. Your responses to the questions are as important as the answers that come to your mind. Journal your responses. Journal your answers. Write. That is your task. Breathe, stay on the inside, write.

In the beginning was the word ...

What do you think of the words on the page? *Tell yourself the passing truth.*

What's your immediate response?

How do you feel about those words?

Are they fair?

Where do the words land in your body?

What do you say to those words?

Write your immediate responses to these words.

One by one ...

Take the words one by one, give them a page to themselves.

Off the top of your head, write what this word means to you.

Keep writing. Whether positive or negative, spill the burden of this word onto the page.

And now ...

Perhaps you've journeyed far enough this day. If you're going to leave us here, remember to journal three things you love, remind yourself why, as you make ready to return to the world of today.

If you're travelling on ...

The word.

What do you say *to* this word? What is your reply?

How has this word shaped your relationships with these people?

Do you live up to the word? How?

Does this word pressure you to play a role for others? How? Who?

Are you threatened? Angry? Diminished? Happy? Tearful? Pressured?

Dive in deeply, how is your life shaped by the word?

What are you required to be for others?

Is this a role you enjoy?

The word 'they' use to describe you – whose face/s do you see?

What is your story of this person or group of people?

Where does the word live in your body?

Does this word shame you? How?

Has this word limited you? How?

What people and situations do you avoid as a result of the word?

Has this word exiled you from the tribal hearth? How does this feel?

Has this word trapped you at the tribal hearth?

How has this word affected your ability to look others in the eye?

Who do you think people see when they use this word to describe you?

Who are you to them? What role are they inviting you to play?

Do you live up to the word? How?

What is your word for them?

What are the stories that come with the word? Events, situations, encounters?

What role do you play in the stories? How does the role you think you play differ from the role others have allocated to you?

Do you need them to be the word?

How does it save you?

Write, write the story of the one word.

War stories

The word is a phantom. A weapon. To be deployed in times of war. The word is a ghost. A wraith in the shadows. The word is a rope with which to bind you to the stories and unconscious needs of others.

How much power are you willing to forfeit to old wars?

As an act of impotent self-protection or defiant self-defence you will have words for others. Words you have weaponised. Words whose power you have timed for maximum destruction. Words that have imploded taking you down with them. Words that have exploded, blowing up much, much more than you bargained for. Words are power and like all sources of power they have their place in the league of right action.

What are the words you have stored for others? Name them. Bring people to mind. Let them come, randomly surfacing to show their face to you. What is your special word for each of them?

Have you journeyed far enough this day? Or are you travelling on? This is your moment to decide. If you are leaving us at this juncture you know what to do: remember what you love before you return to the world you live in today.

And if you are travelling on …

The word …

What damage do you hope to inflict with your word?

Are you using your word before they have a chance to use theirs?

What are you protecting yourself from? Who is out to get you? Why? What did you do to them?

What do you think *they* think you did to them? Did you?

What role do you need them to play for you? If they are (your word) then

I am … ?

What did you fear they would take from you? What would they get that was rightfully yours?

Spill your war stories onto the page. Write from the mind. Then, breathing deeply, feet on the ground, write the story as it lives in your body. Then your heart. What does your heart say about the story?

What is the truth of your story, as best you know it today?

Victors write history. It's your story, tell it any way you like.

An end to the haunting

There is no end to the haunting. Eliminate one wraith from the shadows and another will show its face. This is peeling onion territory, the hall of mirrors game. The best you can do is know the cast of characters in your house, bring them out of the shadows and into the light.

Your task is not to eliminate the word, nor those who use it; *your task is to eliminate its power over you.* Accept you may always be haunted by the word. You may as well make your peace with that. Your task is to surrender stories about the word. Make your peace with that. And this: you have no power over others. They will say what they like. It's their story, they can tell it any way they like. It is you who wears the story like a heavy cloak that is out of season. It is the stories that have power over you, not the word.

Have your notebook and pen at hand. Close your eyes. Breathe. Take up residence on the inside.

And reflect on forgiveness.

We are no longer focussed on the ghosts in your story.

It is you who matters now, only you.

Can you forgive yourself for taking up this story? *No right no wrong no judgement, getting to know the forces that occupy our skin, that's all.*

Big stuff this journey. Are you cooked for today? If you're leaving us now close your eyes and feel the deliciousness of appreciation and agency in your world. None of us is without a glimmer of agency. What do you appreciate? Remind yourself why. And we'll see you when you're ready to pick up the journey again.

Travelling on now, your story ...
  Who are you without this story?
  Can you let them keep telling it?
  What are your stories about yourself?
  What is your word for yourself?
  Is it true?
  What does it mean?
  What else does it mean?
  Are you willing to detach from your stories?
  You have submitted to the roles assigned to you by others. Feel the cascading stories and actions that have resulted from abandoning yourself to these roles. *It doesn't matter why.*
  Feel the abandonment.
  Let the tears come.
  Did you do your best?
  Did you do your best?
  What is your judgement of yourself?

Are you willing to stop playing the roles others have set for you?
No right, no wrong, just tell yourself the passing truth.
There may be roles that serve you – which roles and how?
What was/is in it for you?
Who are you if you are not this?
Are you willing to liberate others from your words for them?
Are you willing to enter the story and make a stand on your own behalf?
Are you attached to the story of the word?
Who are you without the story?
Breathe into the space that comes … let the space be.
Surrender your stories.

Beads of shelter

Our bold, bright spark of a woman in the story at the beginning of this chapter sought shelter from her 'unacceptable' outspoken nature in 'goodness'; paradoxically through the establishment of programs that encouraged others to develop leadership skills. The natural born leader, dying so others might live. Try as she might to seek shelter in acceptability to others, burying her too much spirit in service to others for fear of exile from the tribal hearth, her wild wolf tail constantly slipped into view, the fur matted, unkempt, denied. Ultimately, our wild nature cannot be tamed. Something will break. Break out. Shatter. In our fine example of a woman's case it was her heart. A garden variety heart attack that ought to have killed her; the exploding heart she knew she could attribute to the burden of hiding the truth of her born nature. The mighty oak cannot pretend to be a daisy any more than the wolf can feign lap dog. She sought shelter from the storms of childhood and beyond, raging over and over in her broken heart. She sought shelter in 'service'. Until she broke. And like the wolf out in the rain, she set out across hostile terrain in search of the truth of her own existence.

Got your pen? Feet. Earth. Breathing. Life force, through the skin. There, gently on the inside. Reflect. And write.

Where do you seek shelter from the stories others tell about you?

The clue is inside the roles you play that earn you approval.

Find the threads of these stories.

Where is the point you start pretending?

Where do you deny your true nature?

What is untamed in you?

Why do you hide her?

What do you fear will happen if your tail drops below your skirt?

In your mind's eye find your place around the tribal hearth … what price do you pay for your inclusion? For approval?

The wild one will at first be angry, hostile, as the undomesticated are prone to be when cooped up.

Look deeper. What kind of shelter does she really need?

What is her longing?

What in you is desperate for expression?

Write. Write. Write. Spill the story from your bones, your blood, your flesh, your living spirit.

Now the harder part …

Where do you deny others shelter?

Who do you deny a place at the tribal hearth? Why?

What is her or his greatest strength, hidden beneath the role you have imposed upon her? Was this role initiated by you or have you added your voice to the chorus of others?

Is this story true? Do you have direct experience of this story?

What do you fear from the truth of this person?

Are you willing to surrender your story?

Are you willing to set them free?

Shelter …

Where do you seek shelter?

What power has shame in this story?

What power fear of exile?

Who are you unsheltered?

Are you willing to find new shelter?
Will you play a new role for admittance to this shelter?
Or will you live exposed?

There is no right or wrong in this story. Just knowing what lives in us at this time. That is all, tell yourself the truth of it, as best you know it at this time. Your answers today are not your answers tomorrow.

Shelter. The human heart seeks shelter. The steady commerce of human life is to trade the shelter of one hearth for another. Beads of shelter. Like prayer beads, run through them now. Your sacred beads of shelter. Know your motivations, know your story. Know the truth-this-day of your own heart/h.

The gatekeeper

All of us are born with a super power. It is our greatest strength. Denied it will turn on you, and others. It is the young heart's defence; untrained in adolescence it is the rogue dog who stands to be shot. In untransitioned adulthood it will be the death of us.

What stands between you and bewildering grief?

This is how you know your gatekeeper.

The clue is in 'the one word'. The story burden others have imposed upon you. That toxic tale is your key to your greatest strength.

What stands between you and bewildering grief?

It is a question; answer it.

You already know the answer. It is in the one word. Not necessarily the word itself, though it may be. Look deeper. Inside the word. Deeper. Let the answer come.

What stands between you and bewildering grief?

Like gazing into the waters of a deep pool, let the waters still. You see it below the surface. A little deeper.

There, there. You have it.

Examine it. It is precious. It is that which you have denied. It is matted, unkempt. Mudded and strewn with murky pond weed.

You have it now, in the palm of your hand.

You have it. Hold it. Tender and true. Know this. Feel this.

She is your wild nature, returned.

Lay her gently beside you. Pick up your pen and write.

Write your wild nature.

No questions now, just the familiarity of the one you have denied, returned.

Polish her up, give her shape and colour and form.

Here she is, the wild one who stands between you and bewildering grief. Eating from the palm of your hand.

Write the missing, write the return, write the journey home.

Beyond the word is the gatekeeper …

The gatekeeper is the best of you. She has been waiting for you. She is your secret weapon. Your super power.

She is the cauldron and the fire. She is the sacred sword, hammered, shaped, refined; the mighty arrow, carved and straight; you the warrior who understands, who knows when to hold your fire, the archer who has learned the art of ruthless right action. She is yours to wield. She is the power you distil so finely you might never need to use it, and if you do, when you do, you do so with purpose, striking swiftly, directly, wisely.

She is your responsibility.

All this, from one word. Isn't that wild? An entire theatre production – for what? You might have liberated the word but there are no winners in this game. No freedom when we assume power over others. No gain when we sacrifice our lifeforce to their broken hearts.

Lives shaped by unspoken contracts. The best of us, denied by toxic dance partners. We perform, we pretend, we assign roles to others and readily take up the roles assigned to us. Trading the best of us for validation. For a place by the fire at the tribal hearth. Turning on ourselves as we swallow the storybait of blame and shame. Desperate to be saved from that which we cannot be saved: the fears and shattered hearts of others; their approval and their disapproval, equally deadly; their stories, about ourselves and others. For that is all they are, stories. Fairy tales. Myths we tell to save us from ourselves. Stories imposed upon us that we adopt as our own. Tales we weave from the yarn of wounded hearts. Spells designed to lure others into our theatre, to ensure we're not alone in our illusion.

Know this: if you stay in the theatre, there is no negotiating your place. Fiddling around the edges of the contract is the best you can do. You will barter goods of great value for those of lesser value in return. And if that is the price of your shelter, your place on the inside of the big tent, know it. Eyes wide open.

Use 'the word' to your advantage. Play it up. Live it. Be it. Entertain it like you are the captain and the word is your table. Invite others to dine.

Explore your relationship to your gatekeeper. Cultivate her. She is your strength and you will no longer apologise for her. Know when she is needed and use her. The power within, ready to strike, either on your own behalf or the sake of others. Know this place and learn to dance there. Step up, do not retreat.

And if the theatre is no longer for you, here's what we do. Shhh, come closer, for what follows is a whisper to the one within, the one listening closely, the one willing to leave the theatre all together, the one unwilling to bargain for her shelter.

Here's what we do: we wriggle out of the word like a snake shedding her skin.

Go through the writing exercises again and again and again and tell yourself the burgeoning truth. The word is not who you are. You will not bargain for your shelter. You will cultivate your gatekeeper for she is your greatest strength, your natural born super power, the one who is waiting for you, your dance partner, your love. Let her power brew in your belly. Fire her up. Ready, the moment you need her.

Tell yourself the rock bottom truth. Give the moment you're in everything you've got to give, small as the next breath, large as the mission too big or the vision impossible that is yours to command. Wriggle away, stay close to the Earth, make no apologies for who you are, define yourself according to your own compass. The whole world will not sing your name. It is your own heart that must sing it. Be who you were born to be. That is the law.

12-5 THE BOOK OF THE DARK
Bringing out the bodies

IN THE WORDS of poet and troubadour of the soul Robert Bly, it is absolutely true there is a fix for everything. What is not true is that there is a quick fix, a pill, a healer who can do the work for you. Regardless of your choice of 'healing' – perhaps better described as pathways to health and wellbeing – whether it is writing or otherwise, the work of wellbeing is up to you.

The Book of the Dark is where you meet your mercenaries of shame. The small army of renegade troops for hire that shadow the living heart of you who is doing her best to be good, to keep her head above water, to keep the rest of us from seeing the shame bodies she is hiding in the attic. These mercenaries are the sharp knock at the door in the middle of the night demanding to search the house. The indebted ones loyal only to the paymaster. They are the torturers within. The ones who make you want to die before they find you.

Every human life contains small incidents of shame that reverberate for the duration of our residency. *They see me, they see me and I am not good.* Most human lives include encounters where we did our best and our best was nothing like common gossip good; we fell apart right in front of the unbelieving and possibly joyful eyes of others. *There were witnesses to my crash and burn.* Some human lives become the beating heart of carnage, by accident or design or self-imposed substance-driven harm inflicted upon ourselves and/or others and forever we will disappear beneath the living face of 'that incident'. *I am that and I do not deserve to live.*

I knew a man who was born to a large family in a small village in an isolated rural area in an insignificant country. When he was a small boy he stole a knife. Adults being adults they shamed the child into confession. Now sixty, the man to his own mind is still a thief, shameful and undeserving of a place at the tribal hearth.

I knew a woman who succumbed to the overt and flattering seductions of a young man at work. A diversion from converging tragedies in her life. A 'cougar' pubic hair pinned to the bedhead of a trophy hunter. She died a thousand deaths as she witnessed her shame reflected in cruel pity from the eyes of her colleagues.

I met a woman on a park bench beside a river. We agreed in the way of strangers, looking straight ahead, that it was a beautiful evening. She said she was in town to visit her stepson. Last month's headlines. The man who had shot and killed an accountant, father-of-three. The accountant had stepped in to stop the woman's stepson from beating up a woman at a coffee shop. "Crystal meth," said the woman on the bench by the river, stepmother in shame to the face of murder.

There is a pattern here. Judgement seated on the throne of no mercy. Human beings in retreat. Shamed. Exiled. Unforgiven, perhaps by others, most certainly by themselves.

Shame is the being seen. The hidden heart of self loathing. The absence of mercy. It pushes us to the edge. Demolishes trust. There is no escape. Shame in the shadows, causing us to retreat. Our vile sewer self surfacing, randomly and unbidden, to sting and stink and remind us of the absence of our worth, to revive the story of unsubtle contempt before driving us further into exile.

And if you are brave you will make new shames. If you are brave chances are you will fall. Others will talk about your foolishness with little or zero care or interest in your intention or perceived irrationality. You will be shamed, and judged in the spectacle of your descent.

You will be tempted by exile. If you are brave you will not retreat. You will stand for your courage. You will flex your developing muscles of self forgiveness. You will grow strong. You will rest. You will laugh. You will not rise because now you have your own back you know you did not fall. You did what you did. You entertained the unwilling. You paved the way for the brave who come after you. You risked your all for something *more*. You allowed yourself to be witnessed. You looked the world in the eye. You stared it down. You have a new story. It's yours. Tell it any way you like.

The rules of shame

Our poet Robert Bly says humans have four ways of dealing with shame: we hide, we get angry at seemingly strange moments, we express contempt for others in similar situations, we transfer that shame by shaming others. Who among us has earned the right to sit in judgement of another? I am guilty of all four.

Shame is the absence of love. This, the burning of trust. This, the rise of self loathing.

Self loathing is a terrible, terrible burden. Recovery demands we go to the edge, spill the story, and build trust – in ourselves.

Bly speaks of the distinction between shame and guilt: '*With shame you feel you are an inadequate person. Other people are adequate but I'm not. There's something wrong with me. Everyone knows about my shame and I know it too so the best thing for me to do is go into my room and stay there. I'll come out when I have to and hope I get through this day without embarrassment.*'

Guilt, he says, is not who we are so much as something we have done. You can address guilt. Settle it. With shame, you are the thing that is wrong. '*Shame requires a witness, guilt does not.*'

All that is left to do is love the shamed one on the inside. Offer mercy to the beating heart of courage in others who must stand publicly in their shame. Applaud your own willingness now to venture into the dark to bring out the bodies you have stored in the attic.

Drag them out of the house, down the stairs, through the veiled temple of good and into the light.

Love and truth and death. The holy trinity of courage. The price of one is all three. Every time.

Maybe

There is a parable told in certain circles about a village farmer who had one horse. One night the horse ran away.

"That's bad luck," said the villagers.

"Maybe," he replied.

The following night the horse returned with a herd, which the farmer was able to corral.

"What good luck," said the villagers.

"Maybe," said the man.

The farmer's son broke his leg riding one of the horses.

"Oh that's bad luck," said the villagers.

"Maybe," said the farmer.

War broke out and young men were rounded up for recruitment. The man's son was exempt from conscription.

"Well that was good luck," said the villagers.

Well, we know what our farmer replied. You get the point.

Right or wrong is not ours to judge. Good or bad is cryptic. No human by any objective measure can know all the circumstances and influences and competing interests and demands on a situation, past present or future.

It is only in hindsight that life makes sense. And even then our understanding will shift with the fading light of our passing days, as old stories make way for new and slowly the aggregate comes into focus and we might, if we're lucky, get a glimpse of the whole and be able to say with our final breath: 'so that's what it was for'.

The Book of the Dark

There is no pressure here. No pressure to go anywhere. Just the impulse to walk to the edge and peer into the cavern below. That's all. A willingness to go to the edge, fed up now with old burdens, ready at last to forgo the story.

I have a friend whose motto is FEA. Fucking Enough Already. I have long watched for FEA moments, in myself and others, for it is not until we reach FEA that we have truly had enough of the story we carry – until then, our lives will be on repeat. Same story, round and round. Until you've had enough of the story. FEA. Aaahhh, sweet relief, now we are ready to spill the story, be done with it, lay the burden down and kick it over the edge.

Enough already.

The Book of the Dark is your tell-all. It may take a day, a night, a week, a month. What you will need is a stack of scrap paper or a handful of cheap notebooks. Make sure you have more than one pen. You will need supplies. Food. Water. Warmth. Cushions. A rug. You will need uninterrupted place. A wild headland where the wind can sweep away cloying energies as you pour them onto the page. A forest wherein forgiveness of the living is guaranteed. A river to carry your cares into the cleansing cycle of eternal water. A backyard beneath a wheeling night sky. Outside is your ideal; you will have natural forces for company and a heaven full of radical space in which to disperse the stories that hold disproportionate power over your life. Outside gives you perspective. Inside corrals the stories you'd like to release, humming disbanding energies around the walls; there is a danger you will roast in the residual stench of shame. If you are unable to leave walls for wide open space then open the windows. If you are unable to open windows light candles. You are raising big stories. Old stories. They need somewhere to go. A universe will do.

Which body, where?

The body of shame you begin with is the one right before you, the first one you find. It may be a small story, a big story, a small story with big repercussions. If it's a shame story you've found your first body in the attic. Right there on the surface of your being. It's the story you've had enough of. Fucking Enough Already. FEA.

So gather your supplies. It's an exciting journey. A pilgrimage. A be-gone-now. You may feel dread. If you are honest there is anticipation also. You are making an all or nothing bid to set yourself free from stories that have consumed far more of you than they ever deserved. It is time to bring out the bodies you have hidden in the attic.

Gather your supplies, make your journey to the wild place, and settle in.

Writing the dark

Close your eyes. Summon *The Writer's Breath*. Convene your senses. Tune in to the wild world around you. Earth below. Embed yourself there. Earth, home. The living turning world that is you, inside and out. Blur your boundaries. Comingle your breath. Peace in this place.

Raise your story. Feel its impact on your body as it rises. And write. Write your story. Write it out. Writing everything there is to say about it. The reasonable, the unreasonable, the logical, the illogical, the rational, the irrational, the righteous, the sane and the downright outrageous. Every single thing you have to say about this story, might ever have to say about this story, onto the page. Write and write and write. Write it out. Write it gone. Tell it all. Spill it.

Let the mind have her say, the body and the heart. Hear it all, round and round and round, cutting this way and that. No order. No sense. Just the all and everything of your shame story. Everything. Everything. The world is your witness, pour it out. Cry, rage, tear at your heart, beat your breast. What did you do? Write what you did. What did they do? Write what they did, what she did and he did and then they …

Write. All day write and all night write. The world turns. The sun here, now over there. The shifting light, the moving shadows.

Earth, turning. Waters running. Wind blowing. Grasses growing. Stars wheeling. Give your shame to it all for dissolution and release. Pour it out. Pour it out. Pour it out. Empty your vile sewer self onto the page. Pop the cork on your anger, disappointment, bitter resentments, regrets, remorse, blame, shame. Empty yourself of all that is despicable, loathsome, hateful, hating, hated. Spew all that is hidden, shamed and shaming. Write. Write it out.

The shame. The story. The impact. The new shame stories that set off on their own trail of destruction. The legacy. The release. Write it out. Write it gone. All of it. Gone. Drag out the bodies and kick them over the edge. Watch them fall until they vanish into the transmuting mystery of wild space.

Write until you are done. Ream after ream after ream. Write until you are empty. Until the sweet exhaustion of hard won peace washes through you.

Then rest. Lie back on the Earth. Released. Feel this new body, your body. Feel her new, feel her spaces. Rest, the deep peace of Earth to hold you.

Now open your mouth, gently open your mouth and let what is left of the story fall silently from you. Releasing through the cavernous hollow of your mouth, no longer any hold on your tongue. Releasing now, willingly on its way, glad to be gone into the forever of forgiving ether. No need to speak. Rest, in peace. The story done.

Trust in this place

There is space now. Delicious easy space inside you. And into the space comes trust. Look trust in the eye. Not for another, for yourself. These seeds of trust never left you. Yours by birth. Close your eyes, find them. Feel the tender roots of trust reach into you. Pick up your pen and write them in. Where do they take up residency? Where are the spaces that are theirs to fill? Write your thoughts, your feelings, your tender truth that welcomes trust. No need to push. The growing sprouts have their own intelligence, they know what they are doing. Your peace, their growing conditions; gentle sunshine and sweet, sweet rain.

Taste trust. Feel it. Write what it means to you to trust yourself. You have surrendered rigidity. Relinquished the compulsion to control. You are beyond indignation and defensiveness. There is nothing to defend. No-one can get you now. Trust is rooted in you. You are safe here. You are free.

Breathe deeply. Through the spine. Through your bones. Through your flesh. Your blood. The body gently breathing.

And now dance. Rise to your feet and dance. Beat your feet on the ground in time to the rhythm of Earth and dance. Make a bonfire of your writing if you like and feel the dust of Earth rise as you dance your shame story gone. Dance, feet flat to Earth, breast to the sky and dance. Dance it done.

And when you are ready write your mercy dance. Write your freedom dance. Write your fierce compassion dance. Write your welcome home dance. Dance and write and know the story may have lived in you – it was never you.

12-6 MOTHERLINE
The bond eternal

On enormous and minute wheels of pain and beauty we have turned.
Barbara Mor and Monica Sjöö

A LONG TIME ago I heard this story: a woman goes to the butcher to buy a roast. She asks him to chop off the bone that sticks out at the end. After years of this, one day her daughter asks her why she asks the butcher to cut off the bone. The woman looks surprised. She says she doesn't know.

The older woman asks her mother: "Why do you ask the butcher the cut off the bone?" Her mother says she doesn't know.

So the older woman asks her mother: "Why do you ask the butcher to cut off the bone?"

The great grandmother replied: "Because if you don't, the roast won't fit in the pan."

Family narratives. Whose stories are they? A hundred years ago the pan was too small for the roast. A century later, regardless of the size of the pan, the motherline is still cutting off the bone. Why? *Because unequivocally and unquestionably that's what you do.*

If you have been born, then you can trace your origins back to the first mother. If you have been born of woman, and to date that is all of us, you have been born of Earth. And if you're paying attention, you will know they are the same thing.

There is a tangled net of father lines in each human story – and significantly more fathers and grandfathers than mothers and grandmothers.

There is only one motherline.

If you are a woman, the seeds that would become you grew inside your grandmother's body. *You lived inside your grandmother*. You actually did. Women are born with all the ovum they will release in their lifetime. The first material sign of you was created when your mother was conceived inside your grandmother's body. Track this living genetic material – women giving birth to women giving birth to women giving birth women … and you will find you also lived inside your great grandmother and so on right back up the line. There was never a time when you were not living. You are born of the motherline and even if you do not know her name, their names, you can trace your origins through the line all the way back to the first mother. Her joys, your joys. Her griefs, your grief. Her life, your life. The vibration of her body sounding through time in you.

Her stories, your story.

It's in the way you walk, the way you talk. Your facial expressions. Your longing. Your sense of humour. Your ability to love, your need to turn away. Her lost baby your lost baby. Her survival story, your survival. Her rape your rape. Her laughter your laughter. Her broken heart, yours too. History has its dominant narrative and almost all remembered cultures are an epic of masculine adoration, possession, domination, conquest and the rest. You know this story. We've been swallowing it for millennia. Women have been written out of the narrative. Disappeared. Missing. Silenced. You will never know her story. Others may speak of her. She may tell you something of what she knows herself. You will never know her story because every woman who speaks, speaks for the first time, as if her story has never been spoken before. And therein lies the terror: that one day she might speak. One day she might test the words that tell the story of her living. One day she might tell you her blue thread story*, *what they did to make her stay*. One day we might have to face what is before us and inside us every day. Her story, your story, my living story. Too much to bear.

The west long ago sandblasted reverence for the mothers who came before. We are living a pattern of exile from the tribal heart/h. It is a petty, ignorant version of suttee, the Indian sub-continent rite of widow burning. Ageing women in exile.

Curiously, we have also sandblasted reverence for Earth. The recognition that what we have done to the one who birthed us has also been done to Earth is horrifying. In turning away from the small 'm' mother we have also severed our connection to the capital M. The evidence is all around us. Scoff if you like. Look if you dare. We are born of Earth. Every rock, every tree, every insect, every animal, there you are. Physically, you are of Earth. You emerged from Earth and to Earth you will return. You are an inseparable part of the whole shebang/shebang. You belong to the whole. Like your connection to the woman who birthed you, you are free to turn away. Run, run as far as you like and as fast as you can. The reality is you cannot outrun the motherline and you cannot outrun Earth. You're here and it's time to clean up the small 'm' mess and the capital M nightmare we have unleashed with our denial and destruction of the m/Mother.

It is time to return. Return to the m/Mother. It is time to stop running and face our own beloved face reflected in the ones who birthed us, the m/M to whom we owe life and limb. It is time to fall in love again with Earth. Time to restore reverence for the m/Mother. Time to take a break from our crazy and rest with the m/Mother. Shelter. Sustenance. Renewal. Restoration. Return. Peace in your time.

To give ourselves a living chance at life and we must recognise the injustice of blaming one woman for the crimes of all of time. The tears

---

* The blue thread story can be found in Tracy Chevalier's *The Virgin Blue*.

and the anger and the immeasureable helpless grief – you know it's not yours, yet it lives in you. Honour it. You will never know the story. Whatever is told will only ever be part of it. These are not tales of conquest but survival. You can heal the wounds of the mothers by summoning courage and taking responsibility for all that you are and do and be, imperfectly whole. Here you stand. Living legacy of the motherline. You are her. The not-enough you. Shame and self loathing our bedfellows. Here we stand.

Contrary to common current narratives our power lies not in 'healing' the broken heart. Our strength and our power come from taking up residence inside this space, the vulnerability and heartache ensuring we never forget that we know love: that we loved and we loved well and we love still. Our rite of passage. Our badge of honour. Our re-membering. Nothing to heal here.

Motherline

Family narratives. Hostage to inheritance.

Shall we write?

Grab your notebook, grab a pen. We're going exploring.

Mothercry

Close your eyes. Sitting up straight. Feet to Earth. Breathing. Feet. Earth. Breathing. Ride *The Writer's Breath*, all of life running through you. Connecting now, skin breathing in time to the world breathing all around. Connecting now to the motherline.

Bring to mind your mother. Picture her. Whether you knew her or not. Bring her to mind. Summon her.

What is your mother story? It's a long one, this I know. And if it's short then it's short for a reason. Breathing now. Gentle heart, breathing.

And write. Write your mother story. Not your mother's story. Your mother story. It's a story that may well be told differently every time you tell it. It ought be told differently every time you tell it. The motherline story blows with the wind yet today you have a story.

Write your mother story.

Give yourself a good thirty minutes here. Write what you know. Write what you think. Write what you feel. Write your mother story.

If you're stuck write 'I'm stuck'. *I am stuck on the mother story.* I have nothing to say. Why do I have nothing to say? Drill down. Find your way in. It is there. If you feel empty write *I feel empty.* I have no mother story. I do not know my mother story, aha, so now we have a mother story. Why is the mother story missing?

Write. Pour your mother story onto the page and if not the mother story then your journey to finding the mother story.

Write.

Did you tell yourself the truth as it lives in you this day? Or did you write the story that is the story you can live with this day? No right or wrong here, it's a serious question and best you know the answer. There's a long way to go with this story, and if that's all the juice you have in you, then leave it for now and move into your world. The writing will do its work. You will circle around again, ready to tell a deeper story. We're here, not going anywhere. Let the writing do its work and whenever you're ready, return to write again.

If you are traveling on …

Let's take a deep dive into the mother story.

What follows is a list of questions, for you to explore, a thousand times explore, and you will find new answers, different answers, curious answers, difficult answers, uncomfortable and shocking answers. Remember, whatever you write it's a story. The story that lives in you. We are moving it on and setting it free. Setting you free. Setting your mother free.

Pen, paper, breathing. Feet. Earth. Breathing. On the inside of your skin, gently breathing.

And write, moving up and down the line of questions that follow, for as long as each question takes. Whether your mother is living or no longer, whether you knew her as an adult or lost her as a child or both, whether you knew or never knew the one who birthed you, whether you were raised by a mother other than your birth mother or several mothers other than the one who birthed you. If your place with your mother is secure and without reproach, the questions stand. Your perfect mother is a living woman with living stories written into her source material in the underbelly of her grandmother.

Writing now. Gently meeting the motherline. Writing.

What is the best of your mother?
    What is your mother guilty of?
    Who is your mother?
    Where does your mother story live in your body?
    What broke your mother's heart?
    How are you jealous of your mother?
    Is your mother well and strong? Or does she need you?
    How are you like your mother?
    Are you willing to set your mother free from your story?

What is the best of your mother?
    How do you know this?
    Whose story are you repeating?
    Is this your story of the best of your mother or the family narrative?
    Is it true?
    What is the best of your mother?

What is your mother guilty of?
    What did she do?
    How have you judged her? Write the story of your judgement.
    Is your story true?

What else is she guilty of? Make a list.
How did your mother fail you?
How did she let you down?
How did you feel at the time?
How do you feel about it now?
What should your mother have done differently?
What mistakes did she make?
What is your mother guilty of?

Who is your mother?
When she is not your mother, who is she?
What makes her laugh?
Is she quick to anger?
What does she love?
What does she loathe?
What are her terrors?
Where does she seek shelter?
Where is she vulnerable?
Where is she strong?
Who is your mother?

Your mother, your mother. Let's bring this closer to home. The question to follow is framed 'my', my mother.

Who is my mother to me?
Aaahhh, now we're getting closer.
Sit with this question: who is my mother to me?
Can I bring her closer? Closer. How does the thought of bringing my mother close feel in my body? Where do I feel her in my body? My mother, so close.
Do you need more distance or can you bring your mother close? Can you allow her to visit inside you or is there resistance? Resistance or you want to be ill? Be ill or run for your life? Run for your life or turn around and destroy her?

Writing. You are writing. You are not igniting new stories and old wars. You are writing.

Where does your mother story live in your body?
What is your mother story now?
Write your mother story.

Reasonable or unreasonable, truth or wild accusation, it matters not. What matters is you meet the story within, uncensored, beyond right and wrong, should and should not. The story, as it is in you. The silence, now broken.

Let's keep going. Deep breath. Take a break if you need it. Grab a drink of water. Deep breath. On the inside. And write.

What broke your mother's heart?
What broke her heart?
Do you care? *No right or wrong, no judgement. Just the truth of the moment.*
Do you care what broke your mother's heart?
Have you asked her?
Could you ask? If yes, when? If not, why not?
What broke your mother's mother's heart?
Do you know?
Did you ask?
Do you care to ask?
Did your mother do the best she could or could she have done better?
What should she have done better?
What should she have done instead?
What ought she have done?

How are you jealous of your mother?
What is your immediate response to this question? *Do you stay or do you run?*

Are you jealous of your mother?
What does she have that is rightfully yours?
The attention of others?
Skills, beauty, success, interests?
Where does she suck the air from your world? *Even if she is not living, whether or not you ever knew her, where does your mother story suck the air from your world?*

Is your mother well and strong?
Does she need you?
How do you feel about her needing you or not needing you?
What do you think she should be doing or not doing?
What's it to you?
What's behind your story?
Why do you need your mother to be strong or not strong, to need you or not need you?
Is your mother sick to keep you close?
How do you feel about this?
What is your story about your mother's frail health?
If she is strong and has a sudden bout of sickness, what is the living response in you? *Beyond right and wrong.*
Do you make excuses for your mother? How?
Are you over protective?
Are you neglectful?
What can you not bear to know about your mother?
Are you solicitous in return for … something?
Do you lie to her?
Do you pretend?
Do you fake affection?
Do you love her? *No right no wrong, it's quite the assumption that we must love our parents. What's the passing truth of this for you?*

And now …
How are you like your mother?

For every single question so far, answer this: how are you like your mother?

And after that, how do you feel about yourself that you are like your mother, in some or all or each of these instances – or are you throwing the book across the room right now: *I'M NOTHING LIKE MY FUCKING MOTHER.*

Laugh. It's okay. Laugh. Breathe easy. It's not possible for you to be anything other than like your mother. More than that, for better and for worse, you are your mother. Life's little joke. Haha.

You may as well laugh because here's life's big joke: the more you commit to not being *her* the more you become her. Here's how you know this: *that's what she did.* She ran too. She too was nothing like *her.*

Life, if you are paying attention, is full of small incidents that come about for no other reason than the actions we take to prevent them.

How are you like your mother?

The most important aspect of your response is not the words you might use to respond to this question but the physical sensations that accompany such an innocent question.

How are you like your mother?

Write it out. All of your responses, write them out, pour them onto the page. All the wonder, all the loathing. All the resistance, all the horror. The shame. The sadness. The crazy. The exile. The absolute refusal to forgive yourself/her self.

How are you like your mother?

Writing. *Writing.*

And resting now. Take a breath. Another drink of water.

Feet. Earth. Breathing.

Speaking of forgiveness…

What will you never ever forgive your mother for? Write it out. Pour it out.

What has been the impact of this refusal on your life?

Drill down deeply here.

What has been the impact of refusing to ever forgive your mother?
How has this shaped your life?
Are you being fair to yourself?
Are you willing to tell a different story? *No right or wrong, straight question.*
Are you willing to tell a different story?
Are you willing to let her come in from the cold?
How does the story you tell save you?
Or do you need your mother to rot in slow-burn exile? *No right or wrong, no judgement here, no censorship either.*
How does the story you tell save you the trouble of taking responsibility for your life?
How does the story you tell let you off the hook?
How does the story you tell serve you?
What's another way to tell the story?
Are you willing to drop the story all together?
How is your identity wrapped up in the story?
How does the story excuse you from responsibility for your actions or behaviour?
Imagine your life without this story, how does that feel in your body?
Are you free or are you terrified?
Are you attached to the story or glad to be done with it? *No right or wrong, just the truth of the moment.*

Take a breath. Another drink of water. If you are done here and happy to return another day, then remember to close on a positive. List three things you love in your life and remind yourself why. Write, rest easy, smile. Return to the world as you know it. We're here, you know where to find us. You're welcome, any time.

If you are traveling on …

You are perhaps beginning to understand how big the motherline story. You will need supplies. Grab a snack. Get comfortable. Light a candle for companionship. Or walk it out. Notebook in your pocket take it out to the wild world, take the story to come to the m/Mother.

We step forward into the mother story now as if we are starting again.

Connecting to Earth. Breathing. Writing.

What is your mother's story?

What is the legacy of the family motherline?

What are the stories you have inherited? About yourself? About 'the family'? About life?

Can you do better with the family legacy than your mother has?

Is she yours to judge?

Measure your mother now by her time, place, culture – what ought she have done? *This is not to find excuses for her, or to damn her, it is to do the near-impossible: put a 21st century mind inside the living of another time and place.*

Tell the truth in your measuring. Are you flippant? Are you furious? *The body holds the clues to the limitations of your judgement.*

Do you long for your mother to show you leadership, to show you the way out?

Are you waiting for her to do what you are unwilling to do yourself?

How can you do better than she has done? *Here is the baton; this is your piece.*

Look up from the page. Take in the world around you. Have a drink. Take a breath.

Now we write the mother story as if you are your mother.

Start with three words: I am (her first name).

I am …

And write your mother as if you are your mother.

Your feet, her feet. Your arms, her arms. Your breath, her breath. Your heart, her heart.

Write what she does not speak. Dares not speak. Is too ashamed to speak.

Write what she cannot forgive herself. Write her undeserving, her exile.

Write the masks she wears to avoid your judgement and/or the judgement of others.

As best you can, write your mother as if you are your mother.

Cry your mother home to you, weave a living thread for her to her mother and the ones who came before them. Be her. Live her. Be them. Live them. Their losses, your losses. Their victories, all yours.

I am …

Motherprice

And finally your mother story. None of us escapes the motherline. The mother that is you. Whether you have birthed children or not, you do not get to be a woman in any culture on the Earth without a personal mother story.

Cry now your own mother story. The babies lost. The babies unborn. The babies denied. The babies that were never yours to birth.

Where you did your best. Where you failed. Where you were pressured.

Writing from the body. Breathing deeply, inside your skin. Write gently into the night.

Your personal mother story.

Write.

Where you did your best and to the eyes of others you failed anyway. Where you turned away and still you were left wondering. Where you did what you could in a moment. Where others will never ever know what you did for them. Where you won a great victory and to the eyes of others you were a miserable disaster. Where you lost. Where you mourned. Where you were silenced. Where you were shamed. Where you were exiled. Where your decisions led you now to stand alone. Where you turned left at the fork and you're still wondering about the track to the right. Where youth stole a moment from you and you have been left emptyhanded. Where you have been unforgiving and the burden of guilt was too much. Undeserving when family pride choked you into silence. Family narratives.

What is the motherprice of your place at the family heart/h?

Big story this motherline business. If you're not walking already, it's time. Rug up, hat on, it's time to walk the wheel. Out you go, into the sunshine, into the night. Walk it out. Walk it in. Walk it through.

Make your peace now with the mothers. The ones who have gone before you. Beyond story, there is release. Peace in this place.

Motherlove

Regardless of your mother story, let's remember it's your story and you can tell it any way you like.

You may feel tremendous love for and connection to the motherline. Is it theoretical? A concept? An ephemeral ideal? ... or does it reverberate in your body, deeply grounded in Earth; a no holds barred embrace for your mother and acceptance for the ones who came before; an inside out celebration of what is – or sugarcoated silence? Or you may feel loathing and fury for the one who birthed and failed you, determined to uphold 'the truth' and make her pay and remain unforgiving. *No right no wrong, no judgement.*

There is peace in this place.

Peace in this place is yours for the price of self-forgiveness. Yes, that's the sum of it, there is no-one else to forgive. Any attack we make on another is an assault on ourselves. It is this for which we must make amends and it is here we will find peace.

Would you like to make living peace with the motherline? Are you ready to honour it as sacred? *Perhaps a bridge too far?* Can we speak of the motherline as it is, with no apologies, no excuses, no justifications for actions past? Peace with the motherline. Her living flesh, your living flesh; her broken heart, your broken heart.

Are you ready to acknowledge that no one woman can be blamed for the crimes of humanity? *Beyond denial and defiance.* Can you understand that relief from your pain is to accept the past as no-one's fault? *There is only where you are and to move forward you must start where you are.* It is the story that is painful. Your judgement that is painful. The living legacy in you that is painful.

Are you ready to tell a different story? Can you accept that this different story can be just as true as the 'true' one you are being invited to leave behind?

This is big stuff. You are being invited to drop the threadworn cloak of old stories to make way for something undreamed in you. Are you ready? It's possible this process will leave you naked for a while. If your stories are shared family narratives, particularly a cohesive collusion of the 'what she is like' kind, then shedding the old cloak will leave you somewhat disoriented in your living relationships. Others will wonder why you are silent. They will feel your disconnect from the commonwealth of family stories. They may accuse you of disloyalty or betrayal.

It may take time for you to form a new motherline identity. It could leave you wondering awhile about who you are inside the emerging cloak, not yet formed, weaving a new legend as you rewrite the story of the motherline for the living and offer a retelling for those who are yet to come.

And now …

Notebook. Pen. Deep breath.

It is timely we write a letter to the motherline.

A love letter.

A letter that begins: Dear Mothers,

Quiet now. Light a candle for the motherline. Close your eyes. Slow, gentle breaths. Bring to mind the mothers who have come before you, whether you know their faces or not. There is the mother who birthed you and the one who birthed her and the one who birthed her and the one who birthed her … the motherline, all the way back to the first mother.

Here is your love letter to the line. A letter of all that you know about the living and the ones who came before. A letter from their future. A letter that unfolds your understanding of the line. You are the living one breathing their flesh on the Earth. Write a letter to the ones back up the line. A letter that asks them questions and listens through time for answers. A letter of stories about the forgotten not-forgotten no-longer-forgotten, and the silent silenced silencing now spoken diorama of their lives. Your life. Your letter. A letter that allows for the mysteries of the vast inheritance that is yours.

Your letter your prayer, embedding you in their substance. The further back up the line you go the closer you get to the capital M Mother. Earth. Eventually you reach a time when they were one and the same.

Re-membering.

Write your love letter to the motherline.

It will come from the centre of your body, it is not the province of the mind. *The Writer's Breath* is your ticket in. Breathing, on the inside.

Open your channel to the wild spinning universe and write your love letter to the motherline.

Motherlove. Your story.

Re-turn

Return to the m/Mother.

Here is the lifeline that will save us all for those who are willing to reach for it, embrace it, live it. Turn now and look into her eyes. See what you will yourself not to see.

Breathing. Slow breath. Deep breath. Look her in the eyes. See what has been done to her, perhaps in your name.

See her.

m/mother.

Journal your return.

m/Mother.
Journal the distance you have travelled.
m/Mother.
Write your return to the motherline.

Using The Three Intelligences introduced early in this book, write now. Mind, body, heart. Find your place. Write your place. Belonging now. Sheltered. Safe. On Earth now.

Mother, I am home. Outside. In the sunshine, in the snow, in the rain, in the forests, in the rivers, in the oceans, in the fields, in the mountains.

Of the Earth.

Mother. Belonging.

Write your way home.

> *Earth, alone among the planets,*
> *wills life repeatedly from her own winter.*
>
> Barbara Mor and Monica Sjöö

12-7 THE CRIMES OF OTHERS
Who owes you what and who pays the price

TWENTY YEARS ago, a woman I do not know well was unceremoniously dumped by her lover. They had not been in a relationship long. I know no details of their short affair. All I know is that as is the way of life, one person was in the relationship and the other was out. My guess is the woman I don't know very well endured humiliation, shame, shock, loss, embarrassment, disorientation, the usual responses to the swift actions of others over which we have no control.

Twenty years later, the woman will attend no function where her former lover may be. She will abide no friendship that may overlap between her and the one she has pronounced guilty. Will loudly proclaim 'betrayal!' if a common bond is exposed. Is stressed, anxious and bewildered by those who refuse to exile the former lover from their lives, and severs friendships, new and old, like a vandal lopping off the heads of roses yet to bloom. Her health suffers dreadfully, ranging from high blood pressure to potential explosions in her brain. She is a woman who needs a war. 'I am a loyal woman,' she cries, whilst measuring the worth of those around her by their accession to her 'values', her word. The trouble with high moral ground is that it leads us, and leaves us, a long, long way from home, and our terror resides in knowing that the foundations we believe are supporting us are feeble to non-existent.

I don't need to tell you this is a story of shame and exile. I don't need to tell you that what is missing is forgiveness, not for the lover who abandoned her but for herself, in exacting so high a price for her 'values'.

It is easy to confuse 'values' with punishment and loyalty with blame. *The crimes of everyone but me.* She fears collusion, when in reality the story so gargantuan in her own life has no relevance to anyone else. She fears exposure, when everybody's eyes are elsewhere. She fears isolation ... and there she is. Her challenge is to clear the dust of righteousness and face the lonely light of lucidity. She has been at war with a story and the story is hers alone. And after that, perhaps the greatest challenge of all: making her way back to the communal heart/h.

We all have or have had our version of this or similar stories. Small incidents writ large in the sky of our own reflection, everyday life that does not go our way giving us an endless supply of targets to blame, punishment to be exacted, outrage to express, revenge to plot, wars to wage.

In the 'someone must pay' school of life – that someone will be you.

I know a woman whose earliest memory is waking in the night with her father ejaculating in her face. She was three years old. Her childhood, a mean contest of evasion and mistrust. It was she who tended him when he needed care as he lay dying.

A young man I do not know takes his father's car and drives too fast along a suburban street. He hits and kills a five-year-old boy. The family of the child attends the trial and asks the judge for clemency. 'We have already lost one life,' said the child's father, 'there is no need for a family to lose another. This young man will live with his actions for the rest of his life. That is punishment enough.'

A woman I know is raising children on her own. She took a second job she did not declare to the tax department. A colleague knew she was being paid under the counter and alerted authorities. I was there when an acquaintance said: 'you must want to kill her'. The woman, who was facing trial for a crime that carried up to ten years in prison, looked at her for a long time, as if trying to understand the meaning of the statement. Eventually she said: 'I don't give her a thought.'

Three stories, a hundred lives set free. Three individuals who held considerable power in their human hands, power to shame, power to blame for all that was to come in their lives, power to exile, power to enrage and engage support for a righteous war that would condemn another; three individuals who chose peace instead. Peace for themselves. Peace for their families. Peace for the world in which they live. Three individuals who understood, either by nature or through hard won design, that full responsibility was their ticket through their living nightmare; that shame would condemn them for the actions of another; that blame would destroy them and, ironically, give the one they blamed a kind of defensive leniency; that the mantel of victim would disempower them for as long as it took to regain their dignity. That a legacy of hate given breath on the inside would destroy their families. This is what full responsibility looks like. It does not let the perpetrator off the hook. It sets the one who has been wronged free. Free to live. Free to love. Free to be valuable to others. Free from burdens of shame and exile; in no need of self-forgiveness.

You cannot control the actions of others. Your power lies in what you do with what has been done to you. It's your story. You can tell it any way you like.

Every time we speak, we tell a story. We make up reality. We transfer it to other people. We assess our personal safety in the group by the readiness of others to adopt our story as their own. We measure loyalty by their preparedness to repeat our story to others. Whether we frame our story to reinforce our lack or worth, screen our behaviour or excuse us from responsibility, the story we tell will always be the version that best suits our purposes. Implicit in the story will be the crimes we perceive have been committed against us, as well as warning shots across the bow for the crimes we believe we stand accused.

We are entirely likely to stand with the mob when shame drives a friend or family member or sporting hero or celebrity to ground. Collectively we delight in the crimes of others. Apparent errors of judgement, so easy to see when they are not our own. Their story, our entertainment. Their terror, our rotten tomatoes. Their camouflage, our ridicule. Their exile, our self satisfaction. Their self forgiveness, our shame. That's just one way the story goes.

It is a truism that who tells the best story wins. Stories are the currency of the digital age, the marketing age, the media age, the age of the raconteur and so on, all the way back to the campfire. Stories shape our beliefs and our customs and our actions. They are what we *know* to be true and are no truism at all. Western culture. Story. Modern psychology. Story. Oriental belief systems. Story. History. Story. Religion. Story. Gender. Story. We are at sea in stories. Entire industries, founded on story. There is the obvious: media, publishing, music. The less obvious: medicine, law, politics, science, security. The obscure: families, communities, nations, workplaces.

Everything you know to be true is a story. A story made true by vested interest. A story made true by blind acceptance. A story made true by virtue of inheritance. A story made true by your need for a seat at the communal table. Stories we don't even know are stories, so deeply embedded are we in their 'reality'.

Layered on top of 'reality' are the fiercely competitive narratives that shape our world. *Who tells the best story wins.* They win our money. They win our affection. They win our loyalty. They win our support. They win our vote. They get to dine out at our expense.

'Because' is pivotal to the power of story. The words that follow 'because' determine your ability to enlist others in your story and their ability to rope you into theirs. Stories begin at 'because'. We say 'because' to explain our actions, justify our fears, weave a legend, shore up our ignorance, impose our reality, bind ourselves to a conditional existence and/or mire others in a web of obligation to us. 'Because' is our exit strategy, our excuse, our refusal to take responsibility, our smokescreen, our absence of courage. 'Because' is the point at which you are being manipulated, the point at which you are doing the manipulating. 'Because' makes you right and 'because' makes you small. 'Because' can make you sick. 'Because' can take a nation to war. 'Because' can get you barricaded and abandoned behind barbed wire on a barren island. 'Because' will always speak to the crimes of others.

'I don't have time because he …', 'I can't because she …', 'it's not possible because they …'.

'Because' is a lie. 'Because' is a myth that is about to limit and shape the rest of your life. 'Because' is only ever a small fraction of the story.

Shall we go exploring?

Who owes you what? What crimes have been committed against you? What price are you willing to pay? What price are you paying? Where are you hiding? What are you hiding? Whose story are you telling? In whose interests are you telling it?

Know your story, shape your destiny.

The Crimes of Others

Let's start where we are and have a look at the crimes that have been committed against you: who owes you what, the price you are exacting from them and the price you are paying for their crime. It is too easy to stand by as judge, jury and executioner before the foolishness of others, to throw those rotten tomatoes with the mob in the hope that by mingling with the crowd they won't turn on you. Easier to get excited by the spectacle of public shaming than face the terror that you too stand to be exposed.

Understanding the faces of shame sheltering in your own heart are pivotal to being well and sure-footedness in your world. Walking tall and all that, empowered by the life-giving force of no-one to blame.

Raising your eyes to the eyes of others with the rock solid knowing that you hide no shame.

There are five writing journeys ahead in this section: Behind the veil, Playing the because card, Trigger warnings, Cross purposes trading and Don't read my lips, read my mind.

Before that though, this.

Their biggest crime

Before we begin our journey, let's look at how we're feeling about setting out on our expedition of exploration and recovery.

We'll journal our way to the starting point. Do you have your notebook and pen? A quiet spot on the verandah with the traveling moon will do nicely. Breathing *The Writer's Breath*. Feet to Earth. Breathing. You are about to go in search of shame. Your shame, shrouded by the crimes of others. Your disempowerment, hidden in the folds of your flesh. Your excuses, who might you be without these stories? You will feel physical responses to the idea of coming face to face with the deaths you have died a thousand times.

Working only with the body, breathing softly, deeply, gently. Earth below, sky above, skin breathing the lifeforce that is all around you. Speak through your body. You are setting out to recover your faces of shame. You will need to be brave. You will need to hold your breath steady.

Notebook and pen, writing. Roam through the questions, test them in your body.

You are embarking on a journey towards the crimes of others and the possibility that their crimes are hiding your shame.

How are you feeling about this journey?

Write, write, write. Be honest with yourself.

And now, if you're up for it, write your way forward from here.

What was the crime committed against you?

How are you feeling about shining a light on this crime?

How are you feeling about shining a light on *their* crime?

How are you feeling about shining a light on your shame?

Are you excited? Where is your excitement living in you?

Are you terrified? Where in your beautiful body does the terror live?

Are you nervous? Where in your body do you hold this story?

Do you want to cry?

What do you fear?

Are you relieved by the possibility of mercy?

Are you tense?

Do you know already what you stand to lose by making this journey? Where do you hold this energy in your body?

What do you stand to lose?

Do you really stand to lose? Or do you fear leaving the story behind?

Are you ecstatic at the idea you may be free of your story?

Write your story of the story.

Now we know. Now we are ready to begin. Or not. Perhaps this was enough for you this night. Signing off then with a beautiful thought about what you love in your life. Returning to your world, ready to re-turn again to your place on the page when the stories burrowed into your flesh become too much for you to bear. We are here. Any time.

For the rest of us, it's time to journey on, journey in, journey beyond and journey through and journey round again.

Behind the veil

There will be at least one dominant story in your life. Perhaps you tell it. Perhaps others hold you to it. Perhaps you hold others to it. It might be the homeless story. The child of a dead mother story. The religious cult story. The mean girl story. The sexual abuse story. The 'they didn't understand me' story. The violent father story. The abandoned by my spouse story. The shy story. The depression story. The polite story. The always broke story. The anxiety story. The charming story.

The good girl story. You are looking for a story, small or large, that frames your life. If you can't find a big one for the moment, seek out one that is seemingly insignificant.

I have a friend who is renowned for her patience. And yet the family story of her is an epic of impatience. They serve it up to her like ice-cream on a sunny day, all smiles with a sprinkle of nasty. Perhaps she *was* impatient, forty years ago. The family story pins her to a short period of her life, a child shamed for her impatience. Was it impatience or frustration with the limitations placed upon her? Was it impatience or hunger for life? Was it impatience or a natural quickness of mind and body? Was she impatient or did they feel inadequate around her brightness and quickness? Her crime: impatience. Their crime: shaming her for her brilliance and blaming her for exposing their feelings of inadequacy when they were around her – my friend will be the first to tell you she was not always kind in her quickness. Her response: exile. Her recovery: self-forgiveness. The outcome: peace in her own heart. My friend's family still serves up stories of her impatience, rarely sweetly. She smiles. She laughs. The arrows rush through her skin like dark wind through matter; mostly they do not stick. She holds steady on her feet and in her heart. It's their story, they can tell it any way they like.

Beyond the tiers of dominant stories that shape human lives are the headline stories that are too big for words and beyond the ken of most of us. The mother of a murdered child story. The sole survivor of the family lost in a storm story. The my son shot up the school story. The dingo stole my baby story. Stories that by nature isolate the humans at their epicentre. Stories that carve irreparable fissures into faces and hearts. Stories that expose vast gulfs between the human being at the epicentre of the event and absolutely everyone else. These are events beyond which not a single thing in the world will be familiar or comprehensible ever again. And the rest of us tell their story as if we have just escaped a punch-up at the pub, morning-after conversational currency, trading tales and passing judgements like peanuts at the zoo.

The writing journeys that follow will have value for those among us who count themselves in this rarefied tier of human encounters. However, some of the challenges and prompts that follow may appear trite or even insulting to you, and for this I apologise. The black and white of words on a page cannot convey the heartfelt depth of sorrow shared and care for your pain that would otherwise be present and available were we working together in a room.

Whoever you are, whatever story frames your living, if you are journeying with us, welcome.

Welcome all. Small stories. Big stories. Petty crimes. Big legacies. We are here to understand our own lives. Here to set ourselves free from limitations imposed upon us, by ourselves and others. Here to meet the challenges ahead. Here to be brave.

Welcome.

You have drawn a veil over your face. It is your shelter. It hides aspects of your dominant story you do not want others to see. It is your refuge from the glare of a merciless world. Before we go behind the veil, to visit the mysteries within, we must pay our respects to the obvious. Let's begin by examining what's there for all the world to see.

Breathing now. Writer's Breath. Writing. Cycling through the Three Intelligences as we write. Feet. Earth. Sky.

Briefly, what is the dominant story in your life that's up for exploration at this time?

Your dominant story may be easy to identify. Or it may be hidden amongst an ocean of righteousness or embedded in 'reality', in which case pick at the cloth of your life until a thread comes away. Follow the thread. Any loose end will do.

What's the dominant story you'd like to explore at this time?

Write your story. Tell it straight. Tell it true.

Write the short version of the story? What's a story they tell? A story you tell. You won't have to travel too far from home to find this story.

What's a dominant story that frames your life?

Different people will tell the story different ways. Bring to mind various people and see your light reflected in their face. What story do you read there? They are the screen and you are the projector. What story is playing on their face?

What are the varying versions of the story others tell about you?

What are the assumptions they make about you?

What is your reply?

How does their story impact on your life? *Not necessarily negatively; the impact could as easily be positive, or seemingly positive and still not aligned with who you know yourself to be.*

We have skated over the surface of your story pond. We're no longer skating. From here, take your time. Give the questions that follow your full measure; there may be more to them than you realise at a glance.

Did you catch that? The questions that follow may not be what they seem. The questions are inviting you to look through the words on the surface, much like you might examine a crystal or peer through sheet ice to the living world below. Take time to adjust your eyes. Focus on the unfamiliar. See what you do not want to see.

Still working with a dominant story you tell and/or others tell about you.

The dominant story contains the seeds of at least one crime. The 'what they did to me'.

Writing now. Breathing. Writing, giving each question as much time as you need. Moving on and returning as new information surfaces.

What is their crime?

What did he, she, they do to you?

What is their crime?

How have they shamed you?

Describe these feelings. Spill them. Pour them onto the page. Weep, cry, stamp your rage onto the page.

Where does your shame live in your body?

Where does the shame live?

What is lost to you as a result of their crime?

What is lost?

Who is lost?

Why is this important?

How does their story condemn you?

Your he, she, they story. What did they do to you? What do they do still?

Are you deserving of this story?

Is their story fair or unfair?

Pour it out onto the page.

And now ...

The crime against you inside the dominant story.

Describe how you blame her, him, them for the crime against you?

How have you made her, him, them pay for their crime? *Peering through sheet ice.*

How have you made them pay? *No right no wrong no judgement, just looking at the lay of the land.*

What punishment have you meted out?

Is there an end to their sentence or will they pay for all time? *Sheet ice.*

What has been the impact of the price you have exacted on your life? *Ask your body.*

What is the impact on your relationships?

Your health?

Your everyday wellbeing?

Your work prospects?

Your actions are the proverbial pebble in a pond; the circles radiating out from your actions are the impact.

What has been the impact on the world around you of the price you have demanded as restitution for the crime against you? *Peering through sheet ice.*

Who have you shamed in turn? *Sheet ice.*

What price have others paid for the price you have exacted?

What stories do your children tell that are a retelling – or a reliving – of your story of the crime committed against you?

What wars do they wage that have nothing to do with them?

What stories do your colleagues tell, your acquaintances, your community, your parents, your siblings? *Sheet ice. Pebbles at the bottom of the pond.*

And now ...

We retreat behind the veil.

Here is your shame. The secrets you hold that you may not know yourself. Here is your not-good-enough, your less-than, your unworthy, your they-were-right-all-along, your I'll-get-you-before-you-get-me, your I'll-make-you-pay. Here is your measure of yourself, the one who needs the war, the one you pray they cannot see and yet you know the cause is hopeless, the war your all or nothing bid to divert attention from the shame within.

Notebook, pen, breathing. Feet. Earth. Sky.

Before we journey on, quick check-in: how are you travelling? If you have journeyed far enough this day, be gentle with yourself. Pick up the journey another day. Before you leave us, remember to remember what you love about the world you actually occupy this day. Write out what you love and why, so you might return to your world steady of heart.

And if you are traveling on behind the veil ...

How have you been served by the crime committed against you? *Peering through sheet ice.*

How have you been served by the crime committed against you?

What's in it for you?

Are you off the hook? *Sheet ice.*

How are you off the hook? *Feeling it in your body.*

What is it you do not have to do thanks to this story, their crime?

What are you excused from?

What responsibilities are you relieved of thanks to the story of this crime?

Do you need the people around you to have this story of you? *Peering through sheet ice.*

Do you feel misunderstood? *Explore these feelings. Write, write your mind, your body, your heart.*

Do you feel betrayed? *Explore. Write. Write it out*

Do you feel exposed? *Away you go, pen to the page.*

Breathe. Be sick if you must. Cry if you will. Emptying yourself of the story. Spilling it onto the page.

Looking now ...

At the radiating circles from the pebble that is your story of their crime.

List the emotions and behaviours that radiate out from you in response to the crime against you. *Sheet ice.*

List the emotions: are they are yours? Or are they emotions and behaviours others carry on your behalf, justifiable or not, acceptable or otherwise. List the emotions and behaviours that are integrally connected to the crime against you – hate, loathing, collusion, shaming, terror, nastiness, exile, bitterness, anger, whatever.

Make a list of the emotions and behaviours that radiate out from your crime story pebble. *Sheet ice.*

And now ...

Reparations.

How do you *feel* about your list of emotions?

Remember, feelings are what we feel in the physical body. Feelings are pre-story, pre-emotion.

How do you *feel* about your list of emotions?

Are these emotions what you choose for your life? *No right no wrong, you're seeking the truth of the moment that's all. Another moment, another truth.*

Are you frightened when you could be strong?

Can you be strong now?

Are you angry when you could be laughing?

Can you laugh now?

Are you nasty when you could be kind?

Can you be kind now? *No right no wrong, no judgement. Give yourself a straight answer.*

Are you ... respond to the list of your radiating emotions and behaviours from the top. The question is not are you willing to let them go but can you transform them? If not, why not? And if so, into what?

Do you want to be angry? *Yes! Know your truth this day, tell the truth. No judgement here. No good or bad no right or wrong. If you're going to be it, be it!*

Do you want to be nasty? *Yes, go your hardest. Tell yourself what they deserve.*

Do you want to be strong? *Really?*

Do you want to be free from the dominant story? *No right no wrong, another day you may have another answer.*

And now ...

Are you willing to wipe the crime off the books?

Are you willing to forgive yourself your radiating circles of impact on your life, your family, your workplace, your community?

What does it mean for you to leave the crime right where it is? To carry it no more? To never speak or think or feel it again?

Feel the space around you without this story. Roam around this space. Write the roaming.

The story done. What does that mean?

Done. How will you navigate the energies others are expecting from you?

Done. You are no longer that crime. No longer that story.

What does that mean for your identity?

What does this mean for your relationships?

And now…

Drawing back the veil.

Who are you without the dominant story that has shaped your life?

Who are you without the crime that was committed against you?

Who are you?

How much time have you given this crime?

Did you feature in the crime at all?

Was it personal?

Yes it felt personal, that is not in dispute – was the crime personal?

Examine the dominant story you are working with today. Did they intend to label you shy or was it a throwaway line that stuck? Did your mother die on purpose in order to give you a sense of abandonment? Was your father's aggression fuelled by no other purpose than to destroy you? *Peering through sheet ice.*

How have you lived up to the story constructed by yourself or others? Did you willingly step into the frame others created for you or have you struggled with it *forever*?

What story frames have you constructed for others? For your children? Your parents? Your neighbours? Your colleagues?

Do you need them to be this story?

Why do you need them to be this story?

How is this connected to your dominant story?

How is this connected to your shame?

What's in it for you? *If they are x then phew, I am y.*

And finally …

What's their crime again?

And how has it been your teacher? *Sheet ice.*

What has your story delivered you that you are now able to deliver for yourself?

For others?

Perhaps it taught you survival skills? Perhaps it taught you to be independent when times were tough? Perhaps it taught you …?

Remember my friend renowned for her patience? There is no patience without impatience. The crimes levelled against her and the crimes she committed as she drew battle with her shame became her teacher. Her guide. Her ally on the journey home. The measure of how far she has come. Her apparent impatience equipped her with the vital quickness of thought and spirit she needed to survive on the streets that for a while became her home. It possibly also took her there in the first place. My friend knows her place in their story; and she knows her place in her own story. She no longer needs her family to share or even see her story of herself. She knows what called her away from herself and what brought her home again. It is a story she shares easily with those who are interested. It is a story she never tells the same way twice.

Stories. Crimes. Shame. Blame. Exile. Self-forgiveness. Big stuff this being human.

The veil falls. The wheel turns. We rest. We begin again.

Playing the because card

O. M. G. I dare you to keep count of the number of times in a day you play the 'because' card.

I'm late because …

I need new shoes because …

I can't cook dinner because …

I'm anxious because …
I hurt my ankle because …
I need to get out of this parking fine because …
I have a right to decent internet because …
We need to bomb Syria because …
They have to lock up asylum seekers because …
I have a right to special education for my children because …

Because what? Because he, she, they … what? What precisely do you think you deserve? What exactly did they do to you? This is the petty face of the big material we explored in the previous journey. The everyday excuses we make for our feelings of stress and powerlessness, our overwhelm, our 'it's not fair', our 'this is too much on my own', our flat out refusal to take responsibility for ourselves. 'Because' is the vast mirror of every small and large thing in our world that we believe is ours by right. 'Because' is your unconscious arsenal of blame. 'Because' is the face of your entitlement by virtue of your living. Tough words, I know. Don't take my word for it. If you're up for it, start stalking 'because'.

Your 'because' writing journey is simple. Record the number of times in a day you say 'because'. Make a note of both mundane and more interesting usages. Examine them later, when you have time to rest in the quiet of night. Listen for the hidden messages you broadcast when you play your 'because' card. Listen for the 'because' of others. Watch how their 'because' shunts responsibility, narrows possibilities and shuts down anything at all that might want to be said.

'Because' is your emblematic crossroads. Play the 'because' card blindly and wilfully and by all means get upset when the power goes out (literally and figuratively). If you are willing, fold your 'because' deck and stand by for a new game. Test new words, trial new ideas, taste new language on your tongue. Shelf the need for blame and exercise your courage muscles. The next time the power goes out, light a candle and enjoy the darkness. Eat the ice-cream in the freezer before it melts. Teach the children how to listen to the night. Or stress about it.

Blame 'them', the electricity company, the politicians, the corruption, the 'not getting what you pay for' world over which you have zero control and, according to you, disempowers you. Go your hardest. Stress … light a candle. Stress? Light a candle? You are a grown woman of agency. Stand for your actions without justification, excuse, or even explanation if you don't feel like it. Stress, rage into the powerless dark against 'them', them who can't hear you, are not interested in hearing you – or light a candle and write by the light of the silvery moon.

Trigger warnings

A dear friend of mine is a poet who aimed high and worked hard for banking business success. One night she went along to listen to a well-known songster, a man she admired. Midway through the evening the man spoke of the loss of a child and, to my friend's ears, suggested miscarriage was not the same as the death of a child.

My friend was outraged. She leapt upon her high horse and rode on out of there at full gallop. Ten years later she is still riding, yet to stop her horse for water. His crime: the songster's failure to issue a 'trigger warning'.

What are your thoughts about this simple story?

Grab a notebook and pen. A quiet moment.

What are your thoughts about this story?

Which do you respond to – her demand for a trigger warning or the nature of his comment? Perhaps you relate to my friend's outrage? Perhaps there is another situation in which you know you might react or respond similarly? Or perhaps you have opinions about the value of or need for trigger warnings?

Write your response to this story.

And now …

Turn your attention to the aspect of the story to which you did not immediately respond, the proverbial 'other side'. Write your thoughts. You don't need to do this for long, we're just getting the lay of the land here.

And now ...

Write your responses to the questions that follow. Explore. Watch for the catches in your body, contractions in your breath, surges of righteousness, the breaking of your heart. Remember, this isn't about the either/or of the journey's questions, it's about understanding what lives in you that is quick to rise to the surface, and has the potential to hijack a good night out. Write gently, let your ideas and responses lead you where they will.

What does my friend's demand for trigger warnings, typical for our time, say about us as individuals and as a society? Let's explore.

Breathing. Feet. Earth. Sky. Breathing. Writing

We'll dive in, again by writing your responses to the simple story outlined above. Gently. Your thoughts. Your physical reactions. The story of your heart.

Begin again. Write your responses to the story.

And now ...

Questions that may be more challenging. *No right no wrong, certainly no judgement, let yourself find your way, beyond should and shouldn't. Watch for the twang in your body, shortness of breath, tension in your jaw, the need to run ... watch.*

And retreat if this journey is too much for you this day. Although not before you re-member those three things you love about the life-world to which you are about to re-turn. 1, 2, 3, we are here when you are ready to pick up again.

The questions that follow may be personal for you, they may be academic. Go tenderly if you must. Go boldly if that is your way.

Writing your thoughts ...

The hard question: is the death of a baby the same as a miscarriage?

Does the degree of reverberating trauma depend on the situation or the individual?

This is our starting place. Let's explore more deeply, using this perhaps small, perhaps explosive anecdote *for no other reason than to know ourselves.*

My friend's miscarriage was a long, long time ago. What might be her reasons for being so easily triggered now?

My friend also has a big depression story going. She says it's the reason her husband left her, also a long time ago.

Let me ask you, is depression the reason her husband left her?

My friend is no longer depressed. Yet her depression story frames her story of her success.

How does her depression story serve her? Would my friend be 'successful' if she did not have her 'overcoming depression' story?

Would my friend have her success story if she did not have her 'husband abandoned me' story?

Does she exist if she is not 'depressed', 'an abandoned woman' and a 'woman who lost a baby through miscarriage'?

My friend can be good company. She's clever, and funny. She can also be overbearing, righteous and enraged.

Is my friend seeking shelter? Where? From whom?

Who is she without her stories of what others did to her?

Is her story hers alone?

Does her story make her 'special'?

What 'special' treatment should the rest of us offer to my friend who is 'special'?

What place has shame in this story?

What role has fear of abandonment? Exile?

What acknowledgement or consideration does the rest of humankind owe her, perhaps for the duration of her lifetime?

How brave must a woman be who has experienced miscarriage, a prolonged period of deep sadness and the break-up of a marriage she valued?

If she is less than brave how might she substitute the absence of courage?

Your answers may be short if you do not relate to this unfolding story. They may be long if you do, uncomfortable perhaps, heartbreaking even, maybe even furious with what you may perceive as harshness or heartlessness inside these questions.

What responses are rising in your body as you address these questions?

Ultimately this is a story about you, not my friend. My friend is the screen upon which we've projected our own triggers, our own shelter stories, our own mythmaking.

Check in with the level of energy you have for these questions – are you fierce? Dismissive? Protective? How much energy are you pouring into the story I have told?

Is the story as I've told it worthy of this degree of energy from you?

Or is there another story all together going on in you? What's going on in you?

Write your way through. Keep writing.

We're going to leave my friend here.

Write on if you are drawn to explore your personal triggers, or leave us here if you have had enough for this day.

Remember, write three things you love before you go. Feel each of those three things in your body. Return in peace to the day you have and life that is yours to live.

Ready now to journey on …

What trigger story lives in you and how are you beholden to it?

What is the story you tell over and over. Your ongoing story of bondage, your go-to personal narrative. Use the questions above to dive deeply into the well of your own neverending tale.

What cannot be mentioned in your presence without you either reacting or feeling deeply uncomfortable? *No right no wrong no judgement.*

A word? A phrase? A situation? Experiences?

How do you respond to this trigger?

What do you expect from others relating to this?

Silence? Censorship? Protection? Treading on eggshells in your presence?

How is your trigger a source of power over others for you? *Not whether but how.*

How are others beholden to you through your trigger story?

What impact does this have on your relationships?

Can you make peace with your trigger?

Or do you need other people to save you?

Can you let others off the hook?

Or does your trigger make you special? Fragile? In need of a certain kind of attention?

Perhaps your trigger looks like one thing to others but in reality is code for reminding someone in particular about what she or he or they did to you a long, long time ago?

Are you prepared to have your trigger be your identity for the rest of your life?

Deeper now ...

How does your trigger protect your shame?

How does your trigger shame others?

What would it take for you to come out of hiding?

Are you willing to take the reins of your emotional responses?

Can you let your story evolve with time and maturity?

Are you complicit in your brokenness?

How are you complicit in your brokenness?

Would you be relevant to the world you crave access to without your trigger story? Or is your trigger story your point of connection with human society?

What is asked from you to forgo this story and offer yourself a new one?

Are you willing to forgo your trigger story?

And now...

Do you want to be triggered? *No right no wrong. No judgement.*

If you'd really rather not be triggered, how are you going to manage your surrender?

Are you willing to learn to breathe artfully, so that you might slow down and eventually manage your emotional responses?

Are you willing to forgo dramatic responses? *Maybe you are, maybe you aren't. No right no wrong, no judgement, just turning on the lights.*

Are you ready to have your pain vanish into the wilderness of collective human experience? *Maybe yes, maybe no. No right no wrong.*

And finally...

Amidst all this exploration of what s/he/they did to you – what have you done to others?

Bring to mind one person who has a big story about you, about what you did to them. Who wraps themselves up in a blanket of triggered shame and outrage as a result of something you did, wittingly or not?

What did you do?

What shame do you carry for their shame?

How has this event or situation or incident exiled you from your relationships, including your relationship with yourself?

Can you forgive yourself your actions? Make peace with the one you wronged intentionally or otherwise? Small shames, big shames, they add up to a mountain of unworthy.

This section is an opportunity to examine our own blind influences, the stories, beliefs, judgements and energies that rise swiftly in response to stories disconnected from our own direct experiences. The purpose of this journey is to squint at, stare at, and/or recognise how our responses contribute to, influence and even drive an escalating sense of panic in our ourselves and our communities. We are in new human territory here. With the intensity of our current collective focus on trauma, it is a reality of our times that we pay far more attention to the living broken than we do the living well.

There's every chance in the world the attention and/or visibility we seek requires us to identify with the living broken.

Cross purposes trading

What have you given up in order to control another person? Big question. What have you denied yourself so that someone else is beholden to you? *If I give up x, then s/he can't do y.* The trade might be small: weekends away, a new dress, staying home to cook dinner. The trade might be small with significant consequences: time out with friends, self esteem, bondage. The trade might be huge: university study, travel overseas alone, financial independence. We have a name for this – it is called 'compromise'. I call it cross purposes trading. If you want to broaden the definition, it's a mad cross between archetypal slavery and prostitution, and it doesn't need an externalised 'other' to be shaping your lifeworld.

In a world of perspective, compromise might be: 'okay, we can eat Thai and next week let's do Italian'. Compromise is give and take. It is not betrayal. It does not ask you to forsake your longings and your gifts and the life you are longing to live beyond the fantasy in your mind. Give and take is the healthy trade of human relationships. It is not the demand you give up what matters most, and it does not mandate the sacrifice (and betrayal) of that which you long for. This is not to suggest that everything you desire should be yours, by right, for the asking. It is to explore whether or not and how you make others pay for the crime of your conscious, unconscious and apparently voluntary sacrifice.

Cross purposes trading will compromise you. It is death to the spirit. And there are two possible reasons for choosing this kind of compromise:

1. desperate for a break from responsibility for our own survival, we seek shelter in the life of another and stay too long; and/or
2. we need others to be obligated to us. We need to make them pay. Obligation is our asking price for our sacrifice.

And so we enslave/prostitute ourselves to fear (for example: s/he might leave me) and control (for example: s/he might leave me). We betray ourselves in return for our homes, our lifestyles, our shame, our fear of exile, our absence of self forgiveness and so on. Perhaps you fear your partner's freedom and therefore willingly sacrifice your own? Perhaps you fear your partner's freedom for that would place them beyond your control? Big questions. Perhaps you fear exposure of your shame so better to lie low? Perhaps you fear exile from the communal heart/h so best you stay put? Big questions. *No right, no wrong. No judgement. Living on Earth is in no small part an act of survival. Skip ahead if this is not the journey for you at this time.*

There is a formula for compromise, aka cross purposes trading: *if I don't do x, then she won't do y.* And: *if I do x for you, then you must do y for me.* The crimes of others. The prices we are willing to pay to make sure they pay. Cross purposes trading. Contracting lives. Sharp voices. Breathless hearts. Broken spirits. Lives locked in tandem with everyone doing their best to keep their heads above water, or not. At best, the best of intentions, the doing what's right. At worst, pressure cooker homes. The kind of destruction that lands families in headlines. And somewhere in the middle we find most of us, doing our level best to manage everyday lives with no time to monitor or manage the cross purposes trading, and fear of the unknown one among many of our jailers within.

Are you willing to look? Once visited it's a place you'll revisit a thousand times, with or without your pen. Once you look, there is no unlooking and no turning back, yeah?

If you're traveling on, grab your pen and paper. Find a wild place to rest, even if it's a bench on a busy street. Best not to trap these brave though tender thoughts within walls.

Remember, it's an exploration. A turning over of rocks. A looking at life this way and that. A re-membering.

Breathing now as you close your eyes …

Feet. Earth. Sky. Exhale.

Write.

What have you given up for the life you have now?

What have you given up for the life you have now?

Big question. Write the story then feel it in your body.

How do you feel about this? *Exploring the story, that's all.*

Is there loss? What was lost?

What is lost still? What calls you still of what was lost?

Where does this loss live in you?

Are you at peace with the loss or resigned to it or wildly furious with others for your sacrifice?

What did you believe you would gain in return for what was lost?

Did you get what was due to you?

How do you feel about that?

Feelings are in the body – how does that feel?

Was it worth the trade? *Maybe yes, maybe no, no right no wrong, turning on the lights, that's all.*

With the benefit of hindsight would you make the same trade again?

Or did you sacrifice what mattered to you for an illusion?

Or perhaps you'd make the same trade and manage things differently?

What price have others paid for your trade? *No judgement here, just turning on the lights.*

Have you asked them or are you guessing?

Are you willing to ask them?

Sometimes life is held in equilibrium by what is not spoken. These questions are not to suggest, urge or compel you to crack open this energy field. The sole purpose of this section is to make visible the dynamics that may cause you tension and tears, so you may look at them, that's all, so you may see them for what they are, so you might understand what eludes you and, if you choose, either stay or walk on by in peace.

And now ...

What price have others paid for your trade?
Have you asked them or are you guessing?
Are you willing to ask them?
Would they tell you?
Would they tell you the whole story?
Are you willing to hear the whole story? Are you willing to let them speak? *No right no wrong no judgement.*
Are you willing to share your whole story? Are you willing to speak?
What do you fear would happen?
Are you waiting for someone else to give you what you long for, reparations for your trade and/or the right to speak?
What is the crime at the centre of this dynamic?
What did they do?
What did you fear would happen if you had not made the trade?

Ultimately, no matter which way you turn these questions, when you look what you traded square in the eye, you will be left with three questions and these questions are yours and yours alone:

What shame am I hiding?
What do I fear will happen if I stop trading?
Am I willing to return to myself the gifts I have sacrificed? (These would be the longing in your heart, your deepest desire, your outstanding business in this life.)
Writing. *Remember you are writing.*

It is important to observe the judgements that rise in you as you explore the trades you've made in your life. *We all make trades.* We are not looking at what society thinks of you, but what lives in you as a result of the trades you have made and the impact of your trades on yourself and others. The point of this journey is recognising that it doesn't matter what you trade, or even that you do, what matters is that if you are going to trade, you trade freely, with open eyes, in peace.

Don't read my lips, read my mind

I know a woman who was bottled-up furious with her husband for years about the ease with which he went hiking on weekends, cycling on week nights, skiing at international resorts. She wasn't concerned about what he did; she waved him off with goodwill. She welcomed the time to herself. If she was honest, which she eventually was, she gobsmackingly envied him his freedom. His crime was his failure to give her permission to do the same thing. It was a good decade after their children had left home before the woman understood that it was not he, but she who had clipped her wings. That there was nothing at all her husband could offer her that would set her free. That the jailer was within.

Don't read my lips, read my mind.

Here we find the mostly small crimes of others that loom large in human relationships. What we say and what we want: not the same thing. The small everyday incidents of domestic life that become content for comedy writers and build careers for pop psychologists. We laugh as they mock and make merry and reinforce 'reality'.

Then there are the moments we expect others to recognise our needs and deliver us respite. To give us time out. To cook us dinner. To stay home because we are staying home. To save us from ourselves. Their crime: failure to take responsibility for our needs. This is not to minimise or underestimate the power of seemingly small dynamics. Social roles are encoded from birth and beyond, and can exert phenomenal pressure on our lives. Nonetheless, miniscule or gargantuan, the outcome is the same: the only one who can save you is yourself.

This is oft times reflected in two words: 'I'm fine'. Yep, yes, yeah, no everything's great, just fine; and the beating heart beneath is breaking for want of a witness. Until we're no longer fine and the beating heart explodes for want of a witness and lives are shattered and worlds reshaped and that is not necessarily a bad thing. Or until we're no longer fine and the beating heart breaks for want of that witness and we lament the silence of the one we did not hear and lash ourselves and each other for our failure to notice and suffer for it ever more.

Here we find ourselves in a tangle of terrifying human emotion. Movies are wonderful expressions of these moments, for only in North American movies and television series do humans get to speak wholly, speak fully, speak eloquently and concisely; in North American movies they are witnessed, received, reconciled with their own heart and the hearts of those around them. In North American movies they are loved. In North American movies *people claim a voice* (always at the end). Those tears you shed in movies? They are for you.

Movies reflect the wonder of humanness. Non-celluloid lives make for great movies. Non-celluloid lives are the raw matter from which the gold is spun.

We, however, are not celluloid and we not working from scripts.

We are working with the material that has barrelled down through the ages and lives in us, material that has been wrought by our own experiences, and material that has value here and not there and says who anyway; the unspoken let slide and now snowballing, the avalanche to come.

It is too easy to say 'I can't read your mind' when we do not take time to rest easy with another, so they might have time to find the words (or other words) we seek from them. Too easy to turn from the sorrow in her eyes when time has not been taken for the building of trust. Too easy to let slide the signs of her sadness. Too easy to dismiss her attempt to speak when our minds are zipping about like blowflies on a windowsill. Too easy to be too busy; too busy our ticket out from our own unspoken vulnerabilities.

'I can't read your mind.' You lie. You can see perfectly well she needs to speak. The truth is 'I don't have time for you'. Or 'I can't bear your sorrow'. Or 'I am terrified of your vulnerability'. Or 'it's harsh and it hurts'. It's harsh and it hurts anyway. Or, a different kind of power-over: I've been listening too long here; 'your truth-as-righteousness is killing me'.

Tell the yourself the truth of this moment.

Only then can you make a move in the direction you would actually like things to go.

It takes courage not only to allow another speak, but to listen true. Courage to hear her out. Courage to remain uninvested in the words that come. Courage to recognise there are no true words for the heart. Courage to honour vulnerability, our own and others'.

It takes courage to be still and listen. It takes courage to fumble around in the dark for the words. It takes courage to be seen. It takes courage to forgive ourselves for failing to speak true and for failing to listen true. *It takes courage to understand that what was spoken was only a starting place. It takes courage to rise before the one doing all the speaking.*

Some speak and remain shamed for their attempt at the speaking. Some write letters, their words received, misunderstood, pegged in time. Others remain silent and die their words unspoken. Some of course burn up all the oxygen in the room with their endless speaking, binding others to their torrents of gushing 'truth' (usually prefaced with 'my'). A different courage is asked here. Being caught like a deer in headlights for hours and days while someone speaks at you is keeping the awful peace; it is appeasement, it is not listening. It is a silencing of another kind.

Shame. Exile. The absence of self-forgiveness.

What will we do, huh? What will we do?

What will you do?

The writing here is no list of leading questions. Rather, the writing here is an invitation twofold.

Do you have your pen? Paper? Feet to Earth. Closing eyes. Breathing gently.

Firstly…

What would you speak if the conditions were perfectly right for you?

Write it out. The world is still. There is at least one to listen. You are held by grace in this space.

What would you speak if the conditions were perfectly right?

Write it out. Gently write it true.

Secondly…

Who around you needs to speak?

Who do you know needs a witness?

How might you create a world in which the one and ones around you might speak?

Write it out. Write it true.

Rest now, and imagine a life lived inside your gentle words made real.

12-8 WRITING THE BONES
Home is where the bones are

THERE IS a woman who is a fifth-generation farmer on a big piece of land out there in the never-never that is outback Australia. For much of her adult life she avoided the whisperings of the ancestral spirits of 'her' land as they slipped in and out of her consciousness. A little while back, she started to listen. She began following the tracings and the hauntings and the shadows and the signs of the ones who came before, the black-skinned ones who marked the trees and chipped at stones and ranged the songlines of their/her land. The old ones have whistled their way into her heart and whittled away at her values. Whether it is age or ancestral interference that has shifted her perspective on her life, she will never know. What she knows is that she is destined to live the rest of her days with the dilemma of reconciling living dispossession with the privilege of colonisation and inheritance. For she knows it is not the bones of her people lying beneath the dust of her land.

Home is where the bones are.

Where are your people?

You probably, possibly, maybe know who your mother is, your father, perhaps your grandmother, grandfather and perhaps even further down the line. Nonetheless, where are your people? On what lands did they build their lives before greed or disaster or conquest came to strike them down or drive them off? Did they survive the hunger of the Great Famine that killed so many of their kin and community in Ireland as they watched their food shipped to England? Did they survive the Russian Revolution that killed twenty million among their families, neighbours and countryfolk only to be hit by the backwash of Stalin? Did they survive the Nazi camps while all around them were crucified in the fires of world war hell? Did they walk away or were they forced off their land? Did they flee or did they stay? What did they take that was not theirs to take when they found new life, new land? From whom did they take it and at what price?

This is your legacy.

This is your heritage, the pulsing in your blood and bones.

This is your story.

Our story.

The human story on the wheel of life.

What has this to do with writing for wellbeing? Until now, we have been exploring and examining the personal narratives that rock your world, the ones for which you and you alone can take responsibility for the role you play. Now we meet the big stories over which we have little say and no control and yet are a tremendous source of stress, anxiety, tension, conflict, struggle: the living inheritance of the storyworld into which you were born.

There can be no reparations in these big stories.

Our fifth-generation farmer waged a fierce internal battle with the whispering ancients until she understood they would give her no peace until she paid attention. She has no peace still, aware she is to live out the rest of her days distrusted by the farming dynasties that dominate her community, including the now-adults she birthed who will by 'right' inherit 'her' land, all of whom have sensed the shift in her allegiance to their story. Her life the living tension of parallel realities and dual inheritance, as she goes about her days rounding up sheep and veering off along dusty tracks for a haunting or a marking or a shadow or a tracing, knowing these stories will never be reconciled, at least not in her time.

We do not emerge from this Earth as babes into unwritten life. We inherit stories. We are born into dynasties. Every single one of us born into myths, lies, legends, beliefs. Forces in play when you were born into the centre of them, and those forces will play out for significant time to come.

Entire communities of people and living creatures have a paid a price for all that you are and all that you have. What's more, they still are. That's the way of it. Your fencing story, their starvation. Your progress story, their annihilation. Your success story, their loss. Your story of home, their extinction. Your profit, my blood.

I trust you've worked out by now there's no such thing as 'my' values. 'My' story. We are entangled, you and I, unavoidably and inescapably enmeshed in each other's stories. Your story of conquest *is* my story of shame. Your story of 'the past' is my living hell. Your land, my bones. We are inseparable. Bonded in blame and shame and exile. Our realities, aka stories, are irreconcilable. The tensions are burrowed in and taken root. We do our best to 'get on with our lives'. All of us. Getting on with it. Getting on with it. Getting on with it. Until the tension snaps and someone's had enough and the fire takes hold and before we know it we're in the melee all over again. That's the way of it.

And the melee might die down or it might result in a land rights claim and now we're in whole new territory as the old stories rise bringing righteous dynastic anger with them and even in times of peace, in a quiet corner on the inside, we are holding our breath and waiting for the war. All stories are land stories in the end. And all land stories are tension stories. Because that is where the bones are.

Writing the Bones

Are you willing to recognise your reality is a story? It is a story. Your entire reality, a story. Inherited from the time and place and people to whom you were born. The ones to whom you were born gave that story its meaning and whether you have accepted that meaning as your own or rebelled against it, your life has been and is shaped by it. Your role, the part over which you have a modicum of control, is your investment in that meaning.

There are two writing journeys in this section: Chewing on the Bones Not Buried and Home is Where the Bones Are.

Ready to roll?

Chewing on the bones not buried

Using the land metaphor that's not really a metaphor, let's go exploring for the inherited tensions, hidden, unhidden, unbidden, that live in you. This journey may be academic for you for at this time. It may be your living hell. Either way, if you're here you're up for the journey, so grab your pen and paper and a water bottle, find a wild place that connects you to land, even if it's that bench on a busy city street, if a park or a river is inaccessible to you right now. There is living Earth beneath that cement.

Pen, paper. Resting. Breathing. Eyes closed. Breathing. Earth. Feet. Sky. Breathing. Writing.

What's the big story into which you were born?

Write the short version.

It may be so real, you may have never even thought of it as a story. White woman is a story. Wall Street is a story. Fifth generation farmer is a story. Poverty is a story.

What story were you born into?

Write that down.

Next question: what does that story mean?

What does your story mean?

Remember, the story's meaning has been given to it and to you by others, the people to whom you were born and others who are invested in that story – governments, businesses, non-profit organisations …

What meaning have you inherited with your big story? What does the story mean?

What are your thoughts, feelings, opinions about the story and the meaning?

This story you have inherited, have you accepted it? Embraced it? Rejected it? Rebelled against it?

What has been your response to the big story you were born into?
Pride? Tension? Guilt? Love? Shame? Trouble? Exile?
No right. No wrong. Just looking at the story that lives in you.
What behaviours has your story triggered in you?
A list will do, no excuses or justifications. *Observing, that's all.*
What behaviours has this story triggered in others?
Write down the story of the story you have inherited.

Diving more deeply now ...

Notebook, pen, take the questions one by one.
How attached are you to your big story being true?
If you are deeply attached, why? If not, why not?
What's your investment in your story?
How is your identity entirely wrapped up in this story?
Who are you without this story?
Describe how you feel if this was not your story.
Do you need this story to be true?
Who are you if this story were not true?
Do you exist without your inherited big story and its meaning?

Deeper now...

Can you allow others to tell a competing story?
A straight yes or no will do. *No right, no wrong. No judgement here.*
Can you sit peacefully in a room with others who tell a story that is in direct contrast to your own?
Can you sit peacefully in a room with others who tell a story of conflict that directly challenges your story? *They are telling you your story is wrong. They are telling you your people are thieves. They are making accusations that you find abhorrent. They rattle your bones.*
What energies are triggered in your body as you reflect on this?
Write them down. Write it out.

And now ...

Can you let others speak their experience of your story?

Do you need them to be silent?
Do you need their complicity?
Do you need to be right?
Can you let them speak in peace?
Do you need them to be wrong?

The other is angry and blaming you as the representative of all that has gone before – can you hear their story or is it an attack on you? And if it is an attack on you can you let them speak without taking it personally?

Can you let them speak?

And now...

What price have others paid for your story?

Are you willing to look? *No right no wrong. You don't have to look.*

What price have others paid for all that you are and all that you have?

There is always a price. It cannot be any other way.

What price are you paying for your story?

What's the price too high for you?

Deeper now...

Big questions for the big story now.

Whether it's land ownership or poverty, you have been entrusted with the big story legacy of your line.

Are you responsible for keeping the story going?

Do you want to keep the story going or are you tired of the story?

Time and tide will come, if not for you then for another generation. How important is it to you that the story live on?

It can take phenomenal energy to hold onto a story when fighting against forces that have massed against you. How much will you forsake for the sake of this story?

How do you feel about surrendering the story now? *There is no hint that you should surrender your story. It's just a question.*

What changes if you surrender the story?

What changes in your life if you no longer identify with the story you have inherited?

Who are you without this story?

Is shame a part of your big story? Fear of exile?

You may already be in the process of recognising the story legacy is too great a burden, either for you or for others down the line. What emotions do you feel? Guilt? Relief? Loss? Terror? Write them out. Write your story of surrender.

Who are you without your big inherited story?

These are the unburied bones of your life. The aspects of you unrooted in Earth. If you walk away from one story you will walk straight into another; matrixes and holograms and parallel realities that coexist in time and space.

What is asked from you is you make peace with your inherited stories, the bones not buried. Or not. You can blame others for your absence of courage and persecute them for your fears. Or not. The tensions are living. They are irreconcilable. They are yours now. What will you do with them?

Home is where the bones are

Who are your people? And where are their bones?

Where is the land you must tend in your heart? Where are your people? Who are your people who didn't leave? Who stayed to tend the old ones? The old fires? The old bones?

Shhh, be still. Listen. Their songs, your songs. The song of your people. Rooted in the land.

Pen, paper, water bottle, wild place. Feet, Earth. Breathing. Writing.

Who are your people?

Write what you know. We are not speaking now of mother, father. We are speaking way back up the line. What are five generations or ten when there are thousands, way way way back up the line.

Who are your people?

Where is their land?

This land had an old name, before it was a modern nation. The old land. The old country. The home country had a name.

Who are your people and where is their land?

Who would you be if you knew the ones to come would tend your bones?

How would that change how you live your life?

How would you be different if you knew the ones yet to come were listening for you? Lighting candles for you? Thanking you? Honouring you as one back up the line? Heralding your song in their bones?

How would that change how you live your life?

The tides of migration have likely carried you far and near, your people once their people now your people and round the human story goes.

You can hear their songs, beating the Earth, riding the wind. Voices, laments. Listen.

Who are my people and where is their land?

Who are my people and where are their tracks?

Who are my people and where are their bones?

Who are my people and who is tending the bones?

What griefs possess me that I cannot place?

What masks do I wear that I cannot place?

What limits confine me that I cannot place?

What dangers lurk in the shadows of my heart that I cannot place?

The stories of my people, whistling down the line.

And now …

We feel shame where we do not act for ourselves.

Where is your shame about your people?

We choose exile when shame is too much to bear.

How has exile shaped the story of your people?

Who have your people exiled to hide the story of their shame?

Where are the old ones now? The laments of the old ones back up the line, waiting for you to tend their bones? Where are they?

They whisper to you now. Call your spirit on the wind, cry 'come!'

And you turn to follow the summons on the wind, to pay your respects to the bones of the old ones.

Waving the white flag of self-forgiveness, as you pick your way through the minefield of inherited life and make reparations to the living gone.

Writing now, writing the bones of your people. The bones of your story. Now we come to the closest you will ever get to who you are as human.

Write your way home.

12-9 WRITING THE WILD
Come to your senses

THERE IS A reason we spend so much time lost in the stories of others. Reading books, watching movies, scrolling feeds, soaked in disastrous news stories. The time we spend inside other people's stories is phenomenal. Every single one of our million billion trillion dollar industries is underwritten by their ability to lure us into a story, and hold us there for all time. Entire corporate and political dynasties depend on it.

Many mythologies include tales of a period of time when our s/hero stumbles into the lost in the world of 'faery', where promises of everlasting heaven keep our s/hero too long, where a day is an eternity and our s/hero emerges grey haired and bewildered to wander drugged and listless until they find their way back to the path and begin again the quest that was their path.

We can run about our world with our lives immersed in the stories of others, or we can live our own. We can escape from responsibility and hide inside other people's stories, like Lucy Jordan in her daddy's easy chair, living other people's dreams in our imaginations and soaking up promises that were never theirs to make and not ours to keep. *You will never drive through Paris with the warm wind in your hair.* Or we can switch it off. Literally. In our world we can switch it off. And tune in to the world we actually live in.

Close your eyes and think on this: you are among the ancients, the ones who came before you. Cast your mind all the way back up the line to forever. You live in a world whence you know no other life. No story of another human outside the clan of folk among whom you live. You are attuned to the animals in the world around you. *I am she*. The plants and trees upon which you depend. *There I am in the growing things*. Your life synchronised with the bright astral bodies of day and night spinning above and around you. *I am that*. An individualised self? *No such thing*. An 'I' with longing for another life? Unimaginable. A life of 'choice'? Inconceivable. Your world is a world in which there is no other life but your own. No choices to make. No glittering promises of a better life. No despair about your life's 'true purpose'. You know what you need to do and that's what you do. You live on Earth, with Earth, inseparable from Earth. That's who you are and that's what you do.

Come closer now, closer to our times, and recognise that for all of time up to this point you have lived in a world without mirrors and shopfront windows in which to catch a glimpse of yourself, you have existed with nothing to individuate you from the world around you. Who are you in a world with no mirrors? Do you exist? Do you have to be beautiful? Do you need to measure up? Must you obsess about the shape of your nose? Ruin your day because your hair is not perfect? Who are you in a world without mirrors? What freedoms can you enjoy when there is no need to fuss. No concern about being seen without makeup. No need to perform for others. Your life, going about your business. Your focus, the road ahead. *No mirrors to tell you who you are and remind you who you are not*.

Closer now, all the way up to now. If your life is not recorded do you exist? The current generation of children are living lives recorded from the moment they emerge into daylight. Every move they make, recorded, shared, commented upon. A small child I know believes the image in the phone *is* him. That's how he knows who he is. His life is a performance for others. What about you? Do you exist if your image is not reflected in the phone? How harshly do you judge the likeness staring back at you? What does this do to your sense of wellbeing? Are you dependent upon the comments that follow to define you? What if no-one says anything, what does this do to your day?

Did you have a good time if the party was not recorded, shared, commented on? *Your life, unrecorded. Imagine that.*

Animals feel no shame. It's obvious once stated. Animals do not feel shame. No opinion about what others think, no care for your petty opinion of their teeth, their nose, the image you captured of them first thing in the morning. No care for your interjectory opinion about what they did today. Isn't that an extraordinary way of living? To know who you are and what you must do without a single thought for what others think of your living born nature and what that asks from you. Your task is to live and you will live until you do not.

There is a living world around you upon which you are dependent and of which you are a part. This world lives inside you and outside of you. It wants nothing from you. It will take whatever you mete out. It will not judge you, has zero interest in what you think of your reflection in the mirror and has no opinion about whether you watch the sunrise or record it.

In our modern civilisation this world is a backdrop. It is empty space waiting to be filled. The wild awaiting our taming touch. The living to be domesticated according to your individualised version of 'my' life. 'My' life, my right to be uninhibited by and unaffected by and certainly not imposed upon by 'your' life. And from there we sink into repeating cycles of shame and despair, disconnection and exile, feeding these beasts with the industrialised hunger of the burgeoning mental health industry.

Climate change is upon us. It is payday. We cannot afford you to go down and I do not mean financially. Although depending on which dog you feed, there's that too. The greatest challenge facing us right now is how we manage the situation we have created, contributed to, exacerbated and profited from. Yes, that is all of us in the privileged west and the privileged westernised elsewhere. Our planet is recalibrating. It is adapting to the chemical changes we have generated. Look around at everything you own: the more clothes than you can wear in a year in your cupboard, the overload of furniture doubled up in your storage shed, the cupboards filled with appliances you will never use, the fence around your property that proclaims mine mine mine. It was for that. And now we must step up. This is no time to panic. No time to focus on personal trauma that has outrun its time. It is time to step forward and apply our right to choose to be as well as we can be with the resources available to us.

We need you. We need each other to move beyond shame. To come in from the cold of exile. To get real. To show up. To leave the busy and abandon the crazy. Most of us do not face pathological challenges. That is a reality. You face challenges. That is the nature of living on a planet. There are challenges. We are temporary life forms living on a planet. *We are the freaking miracle.* That's the sum total of it. How miserable do you want to be? That's the sum total of it too. *It's a planet.* It's as much of a miracle as if I told you that you lived on Mars. Whether you look at it from the perspective of the scientist or the mystic, it's a miracle. And you're living it. We are living it. Eight billion living-on-a-planet stories. You are not separate. You are not alone. We are a living universe, right here on a planet. The planet is a system. You are a system. We are a system. We need you. Earth doesn't need you to rest, connect, choose wellbeing and sanity – *we* need you to connect and choose wellbeing and sanity. This is no time to bail.

If you are feeling powerless before the great natural forces that have been unleashed at this time, as 'your' water and 'your' land and 'your' lifestyle come under threat, *turn your focus to what you love.* Too trite? Are you *thinking* love or *feeling* love? What do you love? Feel what you love, in your body. What you love may well be under threat. You love your land? Your water? So tend to it – but first: is it land and water you love, or your land and your water? Where's the emphasis? No right, no wrong. We're knowing ourselves, that's all. *No right no wrong no judgement.*

Restoring love to our own lives will restore health to Earth, our home. Shift your focus from what's wrong – with you, with me, with 'them' – to what's beautiful, and you will be a well being regardless of the challenges ahead of you, and when you are a well being you will be strong and when you are strong you will be restored. So too, Earth. Forgive ourselves our humanness, let the shame and fear and exile fall away, and we will be left with nothing else to do but celebrate the wonder of the human spirit and grow our world anew. Come to your senses, fall in love with yourself as a human being walking your time on a planet, and watch in wonder as everything else falls into place.

Writing the Wild

The writing journey ahead asks you to put the phone down. Lay it down. Give yourself respite from performing for others, a break from the busy. There is a world awaiting you and it asks nothing from you. A world that will not judge you. A world that has no opinion about the nature with which you were born. A world that will neither shame nor cast you out. A world that will accept you in your entirety, as you are.

The question is are you willing to experience yourself as acceptable and accepted, as you are? Accept yourself as welcome without conditions. Accept yourself as beyond shame? As belonging. A place at the world hearth.

Come, grab your pen and paper and water bottle and come, the world is waiting for you.

Exercise 1: Connect

Start inside, in your loungeroom, at your kitchen table. Inside. Begin your writing inside. Bring to mind a wild place you love, remembering that the wild place is anywhere that brings you peace, anywhere where you can drink from the running flow of living energy – a park, a headland, a busy bridge peering through the rails to the river below.

Bring to mind your wild place. Picture it. Write what you see in your mind's eye. Write it. Write what you see, all the little details.

Now go there ...
  Go to your wild place. Settle in. Look about you.
  And write.
  Write what you see.

Observe ...
  How do the versions of your story differ, the one you wrote at home and the one you wrote in the wild place?
  How does your remembered story of place vary from your experienced story of place?
  List the ways your stories are different.

Close your eyes and breathe deeply. *The Writer's Breath.* Through the heart. Through the centre. Feet. Earth. Sky. On the inside. Breathing on the inside.
  When you no longer know your physical boundary, when you cannot tell where you end and the world around you begins, when your energy field is greater than your body, gently open your eyes.
  Write what you see.
  Now, write the story of your wild place again.

Pay attention ...
  What do you observe about your story?

Exercise 2: Senses

Take another deep breath. Be still. Breathe. Close your eyes. Come to your centre. Behind your eyes, inside your ribs, on the inside of your skin. Breathing.
  Listen.
  What can you hear?
  List all the sounds you can hear around you.
  All the sounds. Refrain from picking and choosing.
  What can you hear?
  Write down all the sounds you can hear.

What stories do your ears tell of the world around you?
Write the story of your ears.

Another gentle breath …
Close your eyes.
Your skin now.
What can you feel on your skin?
List all the sensations you can feel on your skin.
No picking and choosing, there are no 'better' sensations or 'irrelevant' sensations.
List them all.
Write the story of your skin in this place.

Eyes closed, breathing …
Your feet.
Feel your feet on the Earth.
Take off your shoes.
Feet to Earth.
What stories do your feet tell of this place?
How do your feet experience place?
Write the story of your feet.

Deep breath, closing your eyes …
Coming to centre.
Gently open your eyes, keep the focus soft.
What do you see?
Write what you see with your vision blurred now.
Write what you see from the deeper place.
What is the story of your eyes in this this place?
Write the story of your eyes.

Be still …
How do each of your senses experience light, shadow, movement, colour, texture?
Ears, skin, feet, eyes.

How do your ears experience shadow? How does your skin experience colour? How do your feet experience light? How do your eyes experience texture?

Run through these possibilities over and again. Take your time. Feel your body's experiences of light, shadow, movement, colour, texture.

What do your ears, skin, feet and eyes have to report about the world around you?

Write your story of this place.

Exercise 3: The living

Return to your centre. Breathing gently, inside your skin.
What lives here?
What lives in your wild place?
Who lives here?
Who lives in your wild place?
Keeping your vision soft, cast about for water.
Whether or not you see water, there is a water story in this place.
What is the story of water in this place?
What story water?
Close your eyes.
Where does it run?
Does it run?
Is it underground?
Has it been channelled away?
Your relationship to the water of this place, visible, missing, running in the deep below.

Write your story of water in this place.

If water could speak through you, what would water have to say about this place?

What is water's story of this place?

Keeping your vision soft ...
Cast about the land.

What is the story of land in this place?
What story land?
Close your eyes.
How does the land roll out?
What has been carved up, carved away, reshaped, weathered?
What story the mountain, the field, the park, the road?
What story the land?
Your relationship to the land of this place.
Write your story of land in this place.
If land could speak through you, what would land have to say about this place?
What is land's story of this place?

Keeping your vision soft ...
Cast about for rock and stone.
What is the story of rock in this place?
What story rock?
What story stone?
Close your eyes.
Where are the rocks?
Does they move?
Do they rise, slide, tumble?
Are they gathered up by children, treasures to hold?
What is rock's story here?
Your relationship to the rocks and stones of this place, visible, missing, moving.
Write your story of rock in this place.
If rock could speak through you, what would rock have to say about this place?
What is rock's story of this place?

Keeping your vision soft ...
Who lives here?
Breathing rhythmically, gently.

Who lives here?
Using your senses. Soft heart. Outside mind.
What creatures live in this place?
What creatures ought to live in this place?
What creatures once lived in this place?
Writing the creatures that live in this place.
Tuning in with your senses, ears, soft eyes, skin, feet.
Who lives here and what is their story?
Casting about with your senses.
What story of the living non-human creatures of this place?
Where do they live?
What is their story of water, land and rock?
Where is their food source?
Where is their water?
Where are the communities of other creatures they rely on for mutual habitation?
Are they here?
Where are they?
Write.
Using your senses, write the story of the living of this place.

And now ...
Choose one creature who belongs to or lives on this land.
If this creature could speak through you, what would the creature have to say about this place?
What is here that your creature needs?
Where are its struggles?
Where does life come easy?
What is this creature's story of place?
Write the story. You are the voice of a non-human creature in this moment.

Deeper now ...
How is the creature's story different from your own?

Using your senses, beyond logic and reason and right and wrong, using your senses write your relationship to this creature.

Writing.

Writing the both of you home.

Exercise 4: Reflections

Landscapes have moods. We have relationships with those moods. The same stormy landscape that strikes terror into one heart will excite and liberate another. Languages are loaded with landscape references: we endure storms in our heart, we are blown away, we get cold feet, we have our heads in the clouds, it's raining cats and dogs, we are full of hot air and we have a snowball's chance in hell.

Closing your eyes. Breathing the wild world around you.

Writing.

How are you feeling today?

What is your mood?

How is your mood reflected by the world around you today?

The sunshine. The rain. The clouds. The bright clouds. The dark clouds. The cold you cannot see. The wind you can hear and is visible in the trees and alive on your skin. The heat from which you shelter in the shade.

How are you reflected in the landscape surrounding you?

Breathing ...

How are you reflected in the landscape surrounding you?

How do the wind and the sunshine and the clouds speak for you?

Perhaps it is their absence that calls you out or locks you in?

How are you moved by the world around you this day?

How has this shaped your thoughts, your experience of this day?

How has the world around you influenced your perceptions?

How has the wild place altered your mood this day?

Do you embrace your mood?

Do you struggle with it?

Do you accept it or do you want to be gone from this place?

Write. Write your relationship to the world as you experience it this day.

Your mind may have entered the story by now.

How has your mind's story influenced or differed from the stories of your senses?

How differently do you feel depending on which is in the driver's seat, your mind or your senses?

Write all that is left to write about your story of your relationship to your wild place.

Exercise 5: Revelations

You have been connecting with the wild forces of life all around you.

Breathing. Closing eyes. Writing.

What have the wild forces shown you this day?

What have you learned from the wild world around you?

What have the wild forces taught you today?

Breathing...

Come to your senses.

How are you different after this experience, even if only for a moment?

How are you changed by the wild place?

How has the wild place shaped you this day?

Write.

Come to your senses.

Write your way home.

12-10 RESTORATION
The best of you

YOU ARE AN emissary of life and you are perfect. If you are wondering why you have undertaken this journey, there is your answer. The journey has been long and at times arduous. We are closing in on the wheel. We have explored and excavated and wandered about lands familiar and unknown, the inner landscapes of our world framed by the megaphone voices that call our lives like Saturday afternoons at the races. It is time to bring the journey home. Restoration is upon us.

Restoration.

A solid word on the page, a prayer as it rolls off the tongue.

Restoration is return. Re-turn to source. A re-membering of who you are and what you are doing here. It is turning your attention to what you love and to what matters most to you and giving all of your life to that. Live there. Come alive. Come home. Surrender what does not matter to you in exchange for what does. Health is a process. It is not static. Stop waiting for things to be right before you do what you must do. Not a single other human being can give you a healthy life packed with all the things you love. They cannot save you. They cannot make you happy. Even if they wanted to, they cannot do for you what you are unwilling to do for yourself. And you cannot do it for others. Your business is your life. To live that one life well. To live that one life well is to live in communion with other lives. It is to live your one life according to what matters deeply to you – not what you 'want', but what matters to you. There is no greater gift or living example you could possibly offer the people who share your world.

The measure is not in what your life looks like to others, but how it feels to you.

While we're surrendering what doesn't serve us, let's throw our collective obsession with happiness onto the bonfire. Happiness requires unhappiness, it's the law. There is no happiness without unhappiness. Happiness is a low bar. You are worthy of so much more. Do what you love. Be gentle on yourself. Act for your longing. Work your way through life's challenges head high as the wheel of life spins you down and takes you up again. Have no outstanding business. Tend the campfire. Take full responsibility. Taking full responsibility is not the same as '*my* life I can do what I want'. Your life exists wholly with our lives. Root yourself to Earth and knit your mind to the inside of your skin. Go about your living at the speed of the growing grasses and the sprouting leaves and the uncurling blossoms and the ripening fruit. Can you accuse the apple tree of being unproductive? Year after year, generation after generation, with only the wild spinning universe to drive it. Are you smarter than this? Could you ask more from your life than this?

Here's what your life asks from you: root out shame, do not abandon yourself to exile and offer yourself the care you seek from others.

In every moment of every challenge you have a decision to make – panic or step up. Crumble or take responsibility. Love or exile.

No-one said it would be easy.

Today you are vibrant and strong, tomorrow you are stiff and laid low. A mystery. It could be the weather, it could be your diet. It could be your thoughts. What's on your mind today? You know full well your mind may be the source of the problem; you also know the answer lies not there. Go to the stiff place in your body. What's the matter here? What's the matter? What do I need from me? Bah, no more colonising the lives of others, come home. Divest. Free them so you might be free. We're all just looking for a soft place to land, safe harbour, beads of shelter from the sudden and the shocking and the storms of our own making.

Restoration

The writing exercises in this section are brief in presentation, vast in scope. They are your guides as you summon a final burst of courage: head high, breaking heart to the sunrise, as you meet the best of you. You are about to tend to writing that which is sacred to you. The journeys ahead are worthy of a precious notebook. Notebook, pen, water bottle, cushion, blanket, whatever brings you joy in your writing place. Pack for your journey and we'll see you in the wild place.

Natural born self

You have a natural born self. A living nature with which you were born. She has been weathered and moulded and shaped and bowed and scraped and buried and …

She is the too-much one or the not-enough one; she is trouble for everyone or else too good to be true.

You can be sure your natural born self is inside these kernels of truth. She is alive and not well in the identity imposed upon you. She is an aspect of you that you most likely loathe and either go overboard to live up to or shrivel to avoid. Others can see her. You know they can see her. They have whipped her into the shape they can bear and the role that suits them best.

Here is your shame. Your shame, your hidden light. They are the same.

Obsessing about our true purpose, or anyone else's, is a modern-world indulgence. Look what we do to the children: demanding they 'reach their true potential', school billboards filled with such promises, yet what a world we create for them, limiting their natural born instincts, curtailing their curiosities, setting them up against each other towards some ideological future that is already crumbling; framing their world with the limited vision and unlived potential of the unbrave, the terrified, the stressed and the broken. Yay us.

Your purpose is no mystery. You know what it is. It is that from which you turn. It is that for which our world can supply as many excuses and diagnoses and pharmaceuticals as you need for not stepping towards it. It is that which you impose upon your children, having not the courage to claim it for yourself. There is no judgement here. We are addressing what you say you want, that is all. Any of us would seek relief, release, rapid exit from the extreme challenges life can throw at us. However relief is not at issue, nor is the human longing for release. What is at issue is your future. Inside the dark heart of prolonged periods of challenging living time *is your future*, your natural born self, *as you are*, making ready to rise and claim, without apology, justification or excuse, the mature woman she was born to be.

Your natural born self *is* your true purpose. There you are. Behind the mask, beyond the veil.

She lives.

Let's write her home.

Breath. Feet. Earth. Closing your eyes. *The Writer's Breath*. Earth beneath you, sky above. The wild spinning universe in you and all around you.

Your natural born self.

She is there inside the stories others tell about you.

You know how to take this journey now.

Breathing. On the inside of your skin.

What do others say about you that causes you to cringe or hide or go to your room and die?

They say I am …

They say I am …

They say I am …

The word or words you are looking for will most likely be prefaced by 'too'.

They say I am too …

Now know this: the 'I am too …' is a story about others and it is a journey for another day, if that's how you want to spend your energy.

For now focus on where we are and where we are is the claiming of your natural born self.

Your natural born self. She is the one whom no matter what you do, you cannot overcome. Always present, ever there, *somewhere*. At inopportune moments she will drop her wild wolf tail beneath your skirts. Just when you thought you had her tamed, domesticated, under control.

What it is that lives in you that will not be tamed?

Burrow in, burrow down, she is there, she is there.

She lives.

Your natural born self.

She is alive!

Bring her out now, guide her to the light.

Dust her off. Put a blanket around her. She is safe.

You will protect her.

Write this story.

Write what you know of her.

What does she know and where is she at her best.

Let her breathe. Let her live. Claim her. She is the best of you. Stand for her. Let her in to every vessel of blood and chip of bone, fill your heart and your lungs and fingers and toes with her. Here I am. Here I stand.

She is home.

Write her journey home.

The world stage

No matter who you are, you have a lived a full life. There is something you know more about than just about anyone else. Wisdom, burning bright.

Feet. Earth. Sky. Breathing.

Imagine you are on the world stage. You have an opportunity to speak to the entire world about what you know.

What is the most important insight you'd share right now?

Write your hard-won living wisdom.

Not judgement, for judgement and wisdom cannot live in the same place.

Your living wisdom.

What do you know?

This is not the same as 'what they should do'.

What is your living insight about the world.

Write a letter to the world.

If the world stage is too much for you, try your funeral. What do you know that is important for others to know?

What is your wisdom message for living?

Your message to the world, what is it?

Your message for the ones to come.

What do you know?

Write your message.

A light, for their journey home.

The death of you

You sit around the campfire with your people beneath a dark moon sky. The stars arc above you. There is dust on your skin. Firelight warms your wizened face. Soon you will leave this Earth.

What story would like the children of your world to speak when you are gone? What story do you wish your grandchildren to tell about your life?

Feet. Earth. Sky. Breathing.

Write the story of your life as you would like it told by the children.

This story is a letter to your passing self. Write your letter, the story of your life as you would have lived it, had the living been entirely up to you.

What is outstanding? What is yet to be done?

What has to die so that you might live?

What has been the death of you?

There is still time.
Write the story of your life as you would like it told.
Write your letter home.

Just for the record

Who are you in the dark of night when all around you is sleeping, including you? Where do you go? Who do you visit? Who are you in the whistling chorus of ancient stories that trail us in the modern age like white ribbons from a jet stream?

Just for fun now, without care for whether or not there is such a thing, write your past life story.

Write as if you had one.

Earth. Sky. Breathing.

Write the song of your people, calling you home.

Start with two words: 'I am …'.

Who are you in the stories of days long gone? Where are you? Whose life resonates in you? What stories can you not get enough of?

What in you is alive to the past yet frustrated in your present?

What superpowers do you possess that are hidden in the riddles and rhymes and archetypes of history?

Write your past life story.

Let the tales of yon and yore bring you home.

Write your way home

You are home. Drop your bags at the gate and take a seat on the front steps, the worn exhale of the traveller returned. Tears well in your eyes for the journey complete. Pilgrim. Pilgrim of life. You have found your pole star. You are home.

Rest and gather your spirits. In your bag are your treasures. Souvenirs that landmark the journey home.

Gather up your bag and enter your life. Home now. Ready to begin. Ready to begin again.

Unpack your bag. Sort through your treasures.

Oh look, there is my resistance, bowing reverently to the forces of life. Look! No hands! No need to hold on. And here! My shame, look at her! glowing bright with the transformation of courage. She is yours to love. And there, there my exile. Oh beloved exile, thank you for the journey. It was all for you. All for you. Thank you, I am home.

You notice your altar of regret, in the far corner, unkempt for once. You sweep it away with a backward glance. You create a new altar, your treasures where you can see them, your natural born self the centrepiece.

And now we dance.

We dance our victory dance.

Earth. Sky. Breath.

Feel your feet on Earth. They beat at the Earth, keep time with the turning world. Your legs solid, your arms raised high. You are home.

Write your victory dance.

A love letter. A welcome home.

Write the song of your people as it sings in you. Your song is our song too.

Sing it out for us. Sing it low and sing it high.

What you have learned and what you have found, your treasures, our treasures. Show us. Show the children. Show the living dead. Sing your victory song so we might sing too.

Write it out. Pour it onto the page.

Home now, write your victory song.

12-11 REST
Shhhhhhhhh

FEET UP. CUP of tea. Glass of wine.

Rest.

Like all worthy women, we begin again. But first, we rest.

We are writing our way home. The wheel is turning. We are coming full circle. We are coming to the point at which you might begin the journey again, return to the first chapter and begin, again. You are stronger now. Braver. You know the lay of the land. Experience has emboldened your spirit and awakened your curiosity, pierced you with courage enough to peer into the shadows that frightened you the first time round.

You know you can survive this journey.

First, we rest.

Stare into the fire. Listen to the running stream. You have all the time in the world.

Rest. You are at a fork in the road. You can rest. Or you can resist resting. If you can rest, leave the notebook alone. If you can rest, pull the notebook onto your lap for the easy thoughts that rise, the renegades who would disrupt your rest, the inspiration you'd like to catch.

Resisting rest?

There is work to do.

You know enough now to pick up your pen and begin on your own ...

Stalk your resistance. Write your resistance. Bring it to the page. I am a busy woman in service to others and I have no rest. I am a busy woman in service to others and I need my no time story. I am a busy woman in service to others and I have no identity if I appear to be idle.

What if they don't care?

Have you tried it?

What if they don't care?

Try it.

Rest.

And see.

What happens.

Here's what happens if you don't rest – no rest, no renewal. It's the law.

No rest, no true service to others. The alternative, that they need you worn down, doesn't bear thinking about.

Rest. It's the law.

12-12 RENEWAL
The force is with you.

WE CREATE OR we destroy. There is no middle ground. This was one of the myriad treasures I brought home from my journey along *The Write Road*. We are either, in any given moment, expanding or we are contracting. Creating or destroying. What impact might this have on our health and wellbeing? What is illness or depression or tension or stress if not contraction/destruction? What is loving and living and cherishing if not expansion/creation?

Take a breath. Is it shallow or is it spacious? Are you expanding or are you contracting? Are you enthusiastic and flourishing or are you tight and stale and shrinking? No right, no wrong, no judgement, no censorship, yeah? Just getting a feel for the lay of the land.

Life is breath. No breath, no life. Creating or destroying. Loving or attacking. Embracing or withholding. Breathing, not breathing. Love or exile. It's the law.

Creativity is actioned longing. It is the driver of the human spirit. It is your source. It is not 'the arts'. The arts is a silo, an industrial whirlpool of demand, judgement, approval, denial, success, vanity, investment, disappointment, success and failure. Your longing to create may find a spark there and it may find applause. But creativity is not competitive. It is not dependent upon the opinions of others. It neither requires nor demands an industry for its expression.

I cannot count the number of times people have said to me 'I am not creative'.

This is a barefaced lie.

I know this because I have witnessed these same people produce a sublime string of words fifteen minutes later.

If you are living human you have longing in your heart. If you are living you can create, you *must* create. You are born to act on your longing. This force is ours by right. It is vital to our survival.

It is *yours*. We all depend on it. Whether you let it flow or hold your finger in the cracks of the swelling dyke, is up to you. That doesn't change the reality you are creative by virtue of your birth.

Actioned longing is your hope and your freedom.

It is there in your fury. It is there in your shattering. It is there on your waking breath. It is your source and it is your living companion. It lives in the abandoned and the weak and the violent and the grieving and the strong.

It asks only that you get out of the way. Stand aside. Let it through. That's all that is asked from you. Stand aside, and let the force flow through you. Let it sweep you off your feet. Let it carry you away.

I know right? Terrifying! I'll say the same to you as I say to the reasoning minds of the ones who come along to *The Write Road* workshops.

So what?

So you're 'scared'. So you're 'unworthy'. So you're 'untalented'. So what?

Birthright. Wellbeing. It is your living obligation.

Over these past ten years I've witnessed countless brave ones quiver in tender terror as tears well in their eyes for the summoning of the courage they need to put three words down on a piece of paper. Three, twenty-three, a hundred and three beautiful words that pour through each individual in our circle onto an empty page. Their reflection. Their awe. The wonder with which they gaze at those black lines on white paper. And then the miracle: their awe reflected in the faces of the people around them, as they share, tentatively, with fragile hearts and shaking voices, as they share with others the words that came from them.

It is life changing. For all of us. I have witnessed it a thousand times and more and still I am changed by the truth of each human heart given voice in a moment.

I am not overstating the miracle.

There is not a single idea in this book that is not reflected in conversations I have had along *The Write Road*. They are the conversations I wish we were able to have at random moments throughout each and every day. They are the conversations that need space to emerge. Humans with longing that speaks, ears that listen, lips that do not rush to judgement and hearts that recognise the sad glory of other hearts.

Creativity is your private dance with the wild spinning universe. It is your piece. The expression that is yours and yours alone. No-one else can give us what is yours to bring to Earth. It is the true task. The only task. A dance that is yours and the only way to dance it is your way.

Creativity has rhythm. Like the turning Earth that gives us our days and our nights and the traveling moon with her many faces, your creativity is a wild force that has its own cycle of rhythm and rest. She is chaos. She is messy. She cannot be controlled. She will come unbidden and she will come and go as she pleases. Your task is to honour the cycle. Your task is to rest easy when your creativity vanishes and to honour the spark the moment she returns.

Longing is the truth of you. It is not selfish but self-ish. It is your giving. Your living truth. And it has to learn to trust you.

The Declaration

Acting for our longing is restorative. In a crazy-busy world it is your saviour. However no-one is ever going to say to you 'I think you should go paint/write/wander with your head in the clouds/sketch leaves/knit a blanket under the moon/paint a mural on the fence/

smash cups for mosaics/rest with running tide' ... unless they think it'll make you, or them, money. No-one is ever going to give you permission to wander without purpose, abandon them to their own world as you explore, experiment, make mess, play loud music, make a nest on a hillside and stay away until it pleases you to return. It is you who must step up to this task. And by far and away it's the most difficult ask that will be demanded from you as you pull your finger from the welling dyke. This is the moment lives change. The stepping forward. The claiming. The kind of courage that is unique among the nations of courage. The one step forward. That one step. One step on this fork in the road and there you go, a whole new direction, a whole new view, a whole other world. Unaccountably yours. Beholden to none but your own living spirit.

Here is the only world of any true value as you make your way towards visibility, here on Earth.

And the paradox, the beautiful paradox: what you do for yourself, you do for others. You lead the way. Your creativity, their permission. Your wonder, their seeds of courage.

And so our final writing exercise on the writing for wellbeing wheel of life is not a writing exercise at all, but a declaration.

The declaration of a Sacred Day. Your sacred day. The restoration of your actioned longing in our world. A day to mark the falling in love with ourselves, as we are.

Our final process is a call to action: the institution of sacred time-out for you in your everyday life. It might be fifteen minutes to start with if circumstances that are *un*imagined frame your life; it might be an entire day each week for the bold and the Fucking Enough Already. FEA.

Our Sacred Day is a day of renewal. And of course few of us will wake up and change our lives overnight. What follows are seven steps that will lead you to the establishment of your Sacred Day; to the restoration of your living truth; to a changing of the guard in your heart and the full expression of your magnificence.

The 7 Gateways to a Sacred Day

Gateway 1: Claim it!

Not a single soul on Earth can give you the time you crave to restore, rest, renew, allow for new possibilities. No-one can give you the time you need to rest with the longing or go wild with the paint.

If you either seek or need permission, you are not ready or willing to claim your living expression for yourself. Even if 'they' could 'give' you that permission, and even if 'they' did 'give' you the time out you yearn for, you would find other things to do with it, anything at all to avoid going *there*. And odds on if they did give it to you, you would be annoyed with them for interfering in your life.

That longing in your heart is hope's promise of fulfilment. Alternatively, it is wishing and wishing invariably puts off what you most desire for another day. That's what wishing is; it is wanting for what you do not have and it is futile.

Sacred time out restores your spirits.

It is the key to your heart's desires.

It is food for your soul. It is death otherwise. Expanding or contracting. Thriving or shrivelling.

The responsibility for its expression is yours.

Yours alone.

Claim it!

Gateway 2: Decry distractions

The needs of others, both real and perceived, will always compete for your time.

Real needs can be prioritised and dealt with methodically. They demand from you the belief there is always a solution. This is your creativity in action.

Perceived needs are tests of your commitment to the wellbeing of your psyche. Perceived needs are the 'they can't get along without me' voices that rule your head and inhibit not just your creative expression, but your promise to yourself and by definition your dedication to the lives of others.

For these are voices of control and shame. You have no choice but to turn your attention from them. They will follow you in, to be sure, to be sure. Your task is to turn away anyway. It is time to take your hands off the wheel and let life go on without you. And it will. The stark awful truth is they can do without you.

This gateway is the biggest and most difficult for women to pass. It is the reason the 'great' artists, writers, politicians etc are so rarely women.

Claim time to express your longing and feel the discomfort of immersing yourself in your own world, your own heart, your own spirit. Just feel it. It's okay.

Feel feel feel feel feel it.

Listen to the ugly stories in your head, feel the pain, watch the events that you summon on your own behalf to distract you, and ask: am I going to allow these old wounds and stories to shape the rest of my life?

Because they will.

Merciless, but true.

All the rest of your born days.

They're not going away.

Take a stand for the longing in your heart, decry distractions and give all your attention to what you long for and love to do.

Gateway 3: Gather your tools

What is it, deep in your deepest heart, that you most long to do?

Do you long to write? Paint? Sculpt or build? Breathe quietly and alone? Plan your political career? Sew? Cook? Study according to the laws of your wandering mind? Walk? Travel?

What tools do you need around you to give your creativity its full expression?

Do you have everything you need?

Warning: there is no such thing as the 'perfect' room, pen, book, brush, paint, shoes, cushion, itinerary. 'I can't afford it' is a story. You are boxing with shadows. What do you need? The universe has your back here. What do you need?

Perfection and the pleading of poverty are excuses not to start, or finish.

Gather your tools.

Gateway 4: Create your temple

Everyone needs a sacred space, a place where they can be alone with their thoughts and commune with their deepest heart.

Create your temple.

Or many temples.

Your sacred space might be public space, such as a coffee shop or park. It might be private space, such as a room in your home or space in your head.

You are entitled to sacred space. It is your birthright.

This sacred space is your temple.

Create or find your temple.

Gateway 5: Choose your time

Here's the thing about creativity: it is beyond the constrictions of time, dimension and the needs of others. It is quite rude, really. It is a pulsing force that comes upon you at the most inconvenient times. It will demand your attention and tug at your heart and claw at your mind until you respond – or snap, if you fail to pay attention.

If you really cannot stop what you are doing and respond, find ways to record notes or sketches. Author Jodi Picoult wrote up her arm as she drove her kids to school.

Make notes, decry distractions and commit to the full expression of your longing by making time.

It might be once a week. It might be once a day. It might be all day every day.

Take more time than you think you can spare, for time is like money: there's always enough for what really needs to be done.

Gateway 6: Begin!

OMG, you've arrived!

Welcome!

You are in a new land. Look around. Breathe the rarefied air. Smile a precious smile.

Only you can deliver on the longing in your heart and here you are! Finally, you stand on the doorstep of your own true life, the reason you were born at all.

Tune in.

Sit. Breathe. Dance the ground beneath your feet. Listen. Light candles.

Do whatever is right for you to acknowledge and honour your presence in this sacred space.

Look out at the clear blue sky of your own life. The light on the horizon out there, it is yours, calling you home.

A journey of a thousand miles begins right where you are.

It is your time.

Begin.

Gateway 7: Begin again!

In many ways, this is the most difficult gateway of all. Returning to your sacred space again and again, as if by right, honouring your spirit of longing so deeply you allow yourself this time to wholly inhabit your world, like letting the night forest into the living room.

No excuses. No distractions.

Begin again.

Here at the seventh gateway is your glory and your triumph.

The world awaits you.

Hear that?

We are waiting.

For you.

Reality check

The universe is on your side. Send a clear signal that *this* is your time, and the great heaving forces of life will conspire to work with you. Do not be surprised, however, if you are tested. You will be! You thought you had distractions before? Try now!

And yet …

Commit and the world around you will commit with you.

Commit and the world around you will commit with you.

Commit and the world around you will commit with you.

The advantages of the Sacred Day

(i.e., what's in it for you?)

Those few hours you devote to your own longing will expand into your waking working life. You will find that you no longer need to rush, that time itself is on your side. You will recognise moments that are precious and love them right then, right where you are, inside the moment you're in. You will learn to focus on what matters; you will no longer be easily led from what matters.

Is a person entitled to three consecutive hours of uninterrupted life?

Grow a Mona Lisa smile.

Of course you are.

THE SPIRAL
The 13th step

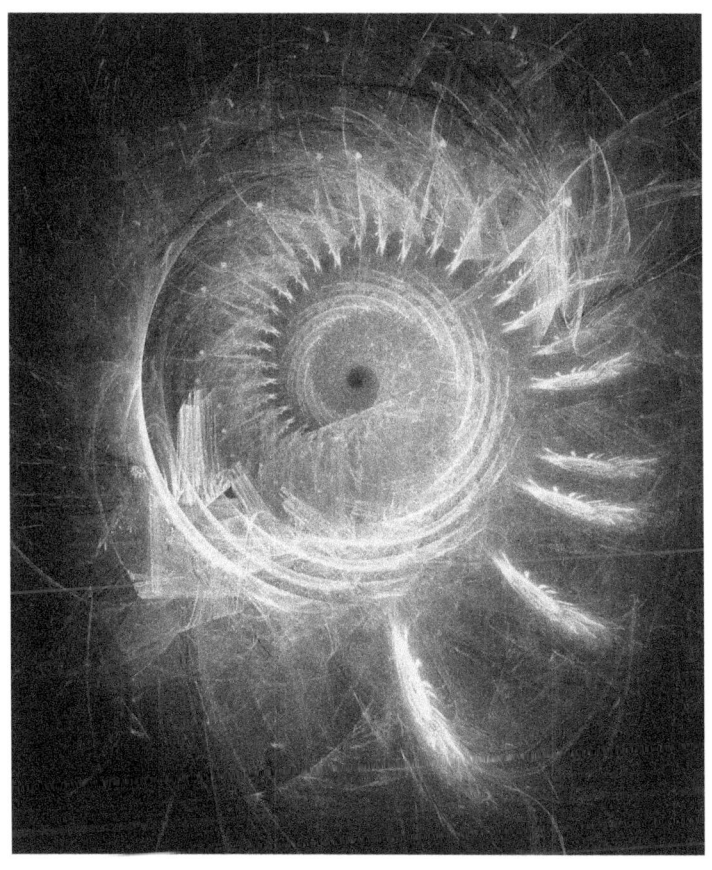

*It is Cosmos to those who know the Way
and Chaos to those who lose it.*

Jill Puree

SPIRAL ON

WELCOME TO the Spiral path.

As you know, *Write Your Way Home* has two parts: The Wheel and The Spiral. The Wheel contains twelve writing journeys, circling around to completion. The Spiral is your one more step, just one, and then another, and another. And another.

The Wheel pertains to the wheel of life, the number 12, symbol of completion, perfectly and wholly divisible by the many. The Spiral is the symbol of evolution, the 13th step, the gone too far, the no going back, the indivisible divisible only by itself and one; the unknown, the timeless spiralling path within and then winding out again only to find ourselves spiralling inward and onward and beyond to curve around again to meet the startling discovery that all of it exists at once.

The Wheel affords us rest, a sense of arrival, the exhale of return, the journey complete. There is no such satisfaction on the Spiral path, no true rest. The Spiral is the path of big courage and its comfort lies in familiarity with the unknown, with making peace with life in its unpredictable entirety. The Wheel is the happy ending. The story that ultimately goes pretty much the way you wanted it to go, albeit with surprises and curved balls thrown in along the way. *It all works out in the end*. The Wheel will strengthen and hearten you, even if only to spin you around again and return you to the same point. The Spiral makes no such promises and the cycling will ever and always derail you in the dark, your illusions raining down like shattered glass, your faith your guide that the light will come again … until you learn the light will not come for you, that it is you who must seek the shifting light; until you learn the light was there all along and that all you seek is within and the light is only the flip side of the dark. No light no dark, just the wild spinning universe, as it is.

The Wheel is the terrain of 'I want'. The Spiral insists on your surrender to what life asks from you. The Wheel offers you insight and comfort, an opportunity to run through the house turning on the lights.

The Spiral demands you unfurl your genius.

The Wheel can be distilled into an approach to living so straightforward it can and ought to be taught to children: problem or solution? You decide. See? Power in your hands, right there. You may not choose the situation, but where you put your attention is entirely up to you.

The distilled question on the Spiral path commands so much more from us, and it is this: wounded or wise?

The seismic shift. The loaded gun. The lost and found.

The Spiral demands full responsibility for the living truth of our existence.

It is a force that compels us into the dark to meet a longing to destroy ourselves so great we may be tempted to dive for the nearest fast track to release. We do not do it. We hold on. We keep going. We hold on even as the world goes on without us and we drift further and further from the common shore. We hold on. The light will come. We emerge into the light. We take the deep reviving breath of the drowning. We live. We take the 13th step. This is the spiral.

This experience has been called the 'dark night of the soul'. It is a journey of reckoning. Nothing will ever be the same again. Love and truth and death, it's a package deal.

Life for the soul-full and the truth-full is at one and the same time a challenge and a song, a gut-wrenching trauma and a dance, a self-destructive murderous plunge and a laugh. The alternative is to go to sleep. Some times in our lives we are stronger than others.

What follows is writing for the brave, for the ones who cannot settle for less than the truth of their own existence, the ones for whom the hand they've been dealt is not enough, the ones who will not die wondering.

You know who you are. You are the ones for whom the passages above make sense.

The Spiral path is full responsibility, for *everything*. No longer fragmented into 'mind body heart' you are now One. One whole being. You will lose your identity. Only to suffer the illusion of recovery before losing it again. The Spiral path is outside time and place. There is no 'return'. Just life, as it is. One phenomenal burst of life.

So there you have it. If walking the Wheel is your way, then write the wheel and return again to the beginning of that section.

Having journeyed the Wheel and you find your heart is rocked by a restless endless timeless longing for *more than this*, then summon your courage and tip yourself onto the Spiral. Either way, write on. And write your way home.

WOUNDED OR WISE

THERE IS GOOD news for our hedonistic times. It's all about you. The bad news? It's all about you. Travel on from here and you will confront your shame in its entirety. The encounter will not be polite. Stand by for a head on collision. You will wrestle your fear of exile in a battle for life or death until you pin her shoulders flat to the ground and stare her right in the face, daring her to keep you from your rightful place at the hearth any longer. You will cross the abyss that threatens to destroy you in a single slip, to find that it asks nothing more from you than forgiveness, for yourself. You will bypass the pitfalls of giving incessant attention to the war stories of the walking wounded. There are no new stories. Only one human story. And from here, only the life you were born to according to your nature. Writing is your ticket in, your ticket through, your ticket out and your ticket beyond. If you need support as you sift through the raw material that is your life, get it! Just know that no one else can get you out of this place. They cannot save you. They cannot forgive you. They can walk with you. They cannot do the work for you.

There is a flag waving in the wind on the far horizon and if you travel the distance you'll find that flag is the flag of abdication from responsibility for your health and wellbeing. There you will find permission to relinquish your strength. To absolve yourself of effort on your own behalf. To abandon hard-won enthusiasm on the funeral pyre of pharmaceutical oblivion. To hand over the keys to your kingdom. (And your wallet.)

In an industrial mindset, we are outsourcing our wellbeing. We can line up all the health professionals the world can deliver to your door, yet if you do not want to be well you will remain unwell. They can work with you. They cannot do it for you. Rather than manufacturing new pathologies, the invitation stands to put the emphasis on the soul of the matter. The soul: that part of us which will assert itself in myriad ways, including the creation of 'health issues', until we *pay attention*. The Greek word for soul, ancient and modern, was/is psyche. Psychology is, quite literally, at its root and its base and its intention, the study of the soul. Could 'mental health' be a menace we've fattened and fed, when all along the psyche has been trying to tell us she's drowning?

Just for a while, let's run with the idea that expressions of torment and restlessness and anguish are not sicknesses to be 'fixed'. Rather, could they be a lamenting call towards a journey that *must* be taken? We deny the soul its natural reckoning at our peril. The soul longs to grow. It's called maturity.

The world will support you to stay broken, indeed the world may be *and is* invested in you being so. It is true, it is true, you will likely be on your own if you grow strong and well. Those Facebook memes that validate your longing to 'be you'? This is the small print. Being 'you' demands change (read maturity). Change, especially self-initiated change, at least in the beginning, can be terrifying. We know there will be a price to pay. We want to know there will be rewards at the end *but we won't know what they are*. The alternative, which is the dominant state of play in our times, is insisting everyone and everything around us to change so that the world is ordered to our small need-of-the-moment. *Nothing asked from me here.*

There is no right and no wrong at these crossroads. We make the decisions we can live with. Either way, our decisions may leave us gasping for air and weeping rivers of sorrow. Then the wheel turns and the world is loaded with sunshine. This is the nature of life. We roll the dice. We do not control outcomes. We don't roll the dice, we do not control outcomes. We can only admit to our awareness the summons within.

The soul longs to grow. When we flatly refuse to allow our soul the deep dive for that which it yearns, we silence and shame and exile the heart of what it is to be human and inevitably this will lead to a health crisis. This journey is vital to the health and maturity of humans, being. It is a grand all or nothing no avoidance bid for the living essence of your one life. This journey is a rite of passage, an initiation.

You are stronger than you know. Step forward. Take the quiet messages of your psyche/soul seriously, before life implodes around you taking you down with it. In this realm there is no double dealing. No crippling compromise. No 'I deserve'. No 'my right to'. No entitlement. No talking your way out. No give way, make way, get out of the way.

Wounded or wise? Wounded and wise.

Writing is soul work.

Let your soul sing.

TRUTH ∞ DEATH ∞ LOVE

Love and truth and death.
You cannot pick and choose between them.
Choose one, you get all three, every time.

THE REMAINING chapters in this book focus on the great mysteries of life, interconnected, inseparable, interwoven: Truth, Death and Love. All of life is a dance with this trinity of power. Whether you know it or not, whether you want to know it or not, love, death and truth are embedded in your living – and they more than likely have you on the run.

In our chapter on Truth we will examine your shame. In Death, we will find your exile. In Love, your self forgiveness. Here, the infinite dance. Here, the irresolvable mystery. Here, the ineffable point of accountability for all that you are.

Here, the lights on recognition that you are not in the stream of life, you are the stream.

13-1 TRUTH

FOR HUMAN beings, truth is a shadow. It is the underside of the leaves playing in the light. It is the coals that warm the fire and burn the flesh. It is the path that humours no choice. It is benign and terrible and when it can no longer be contained, it is the earthquake, the tsunami, the hurricane, the bush fire. Truth, my dears, is elemental.

Honesty, some of us like to say, is the best policy. It is a shared value, as it suits us. Honesty is not the same as truth.

Usually our willingness to be honest depends upon what there is to lose. In reality we can dance with honesty till morning denounces night and darkness returns to claim the light, round and round, but we know, instinctively, that truth is the point of no return.

Honesty is telling your boss you do not enjoy the way he pats your arse in the tearoom. Truth is telling him you can no longer work with him. Either he stops or you go. Honesty flirts with the situation – truth puts it on the table.

Honesty says I don't like it but ...

Truth says I am willing to risk all for my integrity. And, ironically, yours.

Women do not tell the truth. It's been centuries now, millennia even. We hold our tongues and hide the truth of who we are and where we stand, largely because we've forgotten who we are and where we stand. O yes, there are women who rage and spit and lash their fury at an unlistening world. Their expression is no reflection of the words that spill from their mouths, and do not mistake it for truth; it is, rather and always, the madness of grief. They are telling stories to make sense of their loss, for they know they have lost something … they just can't remember what it is. Or was.

Honesty is the emotion of the wounded heart speaking. Truth is the pin-point focus of pure mind, the non-negotiable here, now.

Honesty is malleable, dependent upon time and circumstance. We cannot split hairs with truth.

Honesty is uncomfortable; truth is downright dangerous.

Honesty is a story, a way to define our reality outside of ourselves. Truth is on the inside, the absolute reckoning of self.

Honesty is the child making a courageous stand. Truth is the adult, invincible and vulnerable.

Honesty is gratification; truth has nothing at all to do with what we want.

And that's the frustrating and confronting thing about truth: what we want is irrelevant.

I was working with a writing client, a polite and courageous woman of middle age, a 'good girl' who is about to explode with the absence of authenticity in her life. Authenticity, her word.

She said: 'I claim to value honesty. My whole life is a fucking lie!'

She said: 'I just have to decide what I'm prepared to risk.'

She said: 'I need to choose what changes I'm willing to accept.'

She said: 'I fear everything will change.'

'It will!' I replied.

We roared with laughter.

Here's the fact of my client's matter: it is her immobilised, frightened, tiny, terrified self who is splitting those hairs, taking bets each way, making decisions about choice and risk and loss. Her 'authentic' self, the warrior woman she knows herself to be, will risk anything, including exposure of her shame and the possibility she might lose money, and change everything in order to detonate the chains that bind her. Once surrendered to the 'authentic' path, by which my client means the path that aligns the voices of impossible longing within with her actions, those 'choices' are no longer relevant or even available. *There is no choosing outcomes.* If my client wants authenticity, i.e., the true life that has reached symphonic crescendo in her head and heart, then outcomes are no longer hers to control (as if they ever were). She has only one decision to make: take that one small step towards the light of her own horizon – or not. She knows, if she takes that one small step, everything will change. It has to. It must. That is the law.

The Sacred Unsaid
A dance of seven veils

Well. You're here. You have your notebook and pen. Find the place that gives you a clear channel to the wild world, even if it's just a weed shooting from a crack in the footpath. You are in the territory of the soul now. Take time to practise *The Writer's Breath*. Feet. Earth. Heart. Centre. Inside your skin. Call in The Three Intelligences. This is a whole of body practice. Tell yourself you have nothing to lose by tending to this writing. It is not true. Tell yourself anyway. Or tell yourself the truth. Everything to lose. Everything to gain. No promises.

The writing prompts ahead are short and sweet and simple. Do not underestimate their breadth and depth as you explore your interior world. The questions are your torchlight, it is up to you to take each next step forward.

Know you will meet shame. Your shame. Big shame. Small shames. You are visiting the swamp. You are rooting out shame. Each and every question that follows is speaking to your shame. Dive in. Dive deep. Trace the slimy stems of the vine you find on the surface, down down down to the root. Stir up the mud below. Cry your tears. Beat your chest with your grief. Bellow for what was lost. Go wild for what you did and what was done to you. Plaster your face in mud. Put sticks in your hair.

You will know when you have found your truth.

Your truth does not depend on what others think or say or do in response.

In truth, you have nothing to gain but your freedom.

Rejoice for what is found. Sing for the wonder that nothing was ever lost. The road you have travelled thus far in your life is your work. It is your offering. It is your badge of honour. It is your gift to all who walk this Earth. We need you. We need your experience. We need your recovery. We need you to show up. Here is your courage and here is your more than you know.

First, however, first we must visit the swamp.

These are big journeys. My advice is to take them one by one. At the very least, on the deeper dive, take a break between each question. Look up, immerse yourself in the wild forces all around you, earth, wind, sky, river, trees, birds. Take a break. Or take each question one day at a time, re-entering your everyday world between questions and returning to the pages tomorrow, one big exploration of truth/shame at a time.

Here is the overview. Familiarise yourself with the territory ahead by exploring in writing each of the questions that follow, six of your seven veils, the final veil to be revealed when you get there:

Who are my enemies?
What do I fear?
What do I treasure?
What do I cling to?
What are my alibis?
What is the truth I do not speak?

And now ...

Are you ready for the deeper dive?

Veil 7: Who are my enemies?
Please don't say you have none

Who do you habitually despise? Have something to say about? Put down? Ignore? Roll your eyes at?

Who and/or what is your dumping ground? The person or institution upon whom or which you stockpile your discontent, project your anger, fire your hostility, blame for your broken heart, kill if you have to as recompense for your unresolved trauma and unexposed shame?

Make a list of your enemies. Describe your relationship to each and every one. Drill down into the detail. Write every single thing you think, believe, abhor, loathe, hate, believe, have to say about them. Reasonable and unreasonable, righteous and downright outrageous.

Write it out. Write it all. Spill it.

Closing your eyes ...

Where does this hostility live in your body?

Close your eyes, breathe through your centre. Bring to mind your enemy, your thoughts about her or him or it. Where does this story live in you?

What is its impact on you? Physically? Emotionally? Your soul/psyche?

How is your life restricted by your enemy? What is its impact on your life? Are there places you cannot go? People you do not see? Relationships once valued now diminished? *No right no wrong, no judgement in this place.*

Where do the myriad aspects of your enemy story live in your body? Where has your enemy taken up residence inside you?

How does your enemy influence your life?

How do you feel about this influence?

Writing.

Breathing gently, inside your skin ...

What shame are you hiding behind your enemy?

What are you frightened people will see?

What did your enemy see in you that shamed you?

Are you frightened your enemy was right? That you are that?

Tell your shame story. Tell it now. Spill it. All of it.
Is it true? Are you that?
Dump it onto the page.
Do you believe it?
Is it true? Is that who you are?
Start as many sentences as you can with 'I am ...' and fill in the blanks with the voice of your enemy.
Fill in the blanks with your own vicious voices, anonymous and otherwise.
Empty yourself of the shame voices.
Writing.

And now this ...
Are you willing to release yourself from your enemy's shame?
Are you willing to forgo your enemy shame story? *No right no wrong.*
Who are you without this story? What is required from you? How is your experience of your body different without these shame stories?
Keep writing.

And now this ...
How does your enemy serve you?
Perhaps dumping on this person or institution gives you somewhere to release unbidden tensions and/or unresolved trauma from your past? Perhaps you want to get them before they get you? Perhaps it makes you feel less insecure around them? Are you jealous of this person? Why are you jealous? What do you perceive is lacking in you? Do you feel powerless around them? Do they remind you of someone? Do they remind you of a situation? What does hating your enemy prevent you from addressing in yourself? How does it save you?

And now this ...
Are you willing to release your need for this enemy?
What are your conditions for their release? For your own release?

What steps would you need to take to feel safe/surrender the war?

What physical price are you paying for your enemy story?

How would your life be different if you drop the need for this enemy?

Reading now ...

Read over your thoughts and beliefs and opinions about your enemy/ies.

It's a big story.

It's your big story.

Is what you have written true?

What doubts do you have about your story?

Inside your skin ...

Kindly now, with gentle heart, what do your words say about you?

Forget your enemy, just for the moment if that's all you can bear.

Focus on your beautiful hurting self.

What shames still exist in your story?

Big shames. Awful shames. Do not see me shames. Write them out. Root them out. Haul them out of the swampy slimy shadows, hold them bedraggled and limp up to the light.

Weep for their humiliation and your loss. Love them. Love them.

Diving in now ...

Why the need for the enemy? Do they see too much? 'Make' you feel ...?

Are you willing to set yourself free?

What fears surface with this question?

Are you willing to set yourself free?

Do you want them to pay?

How should they pay and for how long?

For how long are you willing to bind your enemy to you?

Are you willing to be free?

What do you need to do to move forward without them or your story about them?

What space opens out in your life if you let the enemy go?

How are you vulnerable and what steps do you need to take to make yourself strong?

Who are you with your enemy? How does s/he/it give you the illusion of power or strength?

Who are you without your enemy?

Who are you without your enemy?

What angers, jealousies, crippled senses can you justify in your life courtesy of your enemy?

Deeper still ...

Face your enemy now.

The person who is your enemy, the person who represents your enemy if your enemy is an institution. Look them in the eye.

What shames still rise in you as you face your enemy? Are you willing to surrender the shame you feel?

Are you willing to walk away?

Are you willing to forgive yourself the price you have paid for your war?

Are you willing to move forward in your life and let them go in peace?

Are you willing to live without them? *No right, no wrong, no judgement. Just shining a light.*

If you are not willing to walk on without them, how does this impact your life from here?

If you are willing to walk on without them, how does your life demand greater accountability from you, now you are free?

Tell the bedrock truth. Not what is right. Not what is good. Not what is safe. Much, much more than what is honest. Drill down until every cell in your body can sing I have told the truth.

Veil 6: What do I fear?
Farrrrk, are you ready for this one?

What do you fear?

1. Make a list. One long long list of everything you can think of that you fear. Down the page. Off the top of your head. Be honest.
   Being murdered in the dark.
   The plane crashing.
   My partner leaving me.
   My children hating me.
   Getting cancer.
   My father.
   Having no money.
   People hating me.
   No-one will love me.
   That this is all there is in my life.
   Make a list. A long long long list of your personalised fears.
2. Close your eyes. Take each item on your list one by one. Where does each of your fears live in your body? One by one, where do hold the vibration of this fear? Write that next to each fear, one by one, a second column forming on your page.
3. How do you behave as a result of your fear? What is the impact of this fear on your life? How does it limit you? Each fear, one by one. Write a third column.
4. Is this fear reasonable? Add a Y or an N in a fourth column beside each fear, down the page.
5. Is this fear acceptable to you? Y or N. A fifth column down the page.
6. Is the impact on your physical and/or mental health acceptable? Y or N. Sixth column.
7. How does this fear serve you? What responsibilities are you exempt from as a result of your fear? Where are you excused

from showing up in your life thanks to this fear? How does it save you? One line is all that's needed. No exploration. Just one statement. Seventh column.
8. Are you willing to rise above this fear? Y or N. Eighth column.
9. The number of completion. The ninth column is this: what is the source of this fear? The news? Television? Because it happened to someone I know? Social media? A commonwealth of panic? Also known as 'everybody says so'. In a word or three, list the source of your fears.

Now breathe. Look over your page. Here you are. The unbidden, the unspoken, the terrorists on the inside. Here is your reflection, in shorthand, the subterranean currents of your life influencing everything you are and everything you do and everyone you know (terrifying, isn't it?). And these are just the shopfront story fears. Most of them are not even yours. Whose fears are they? All this, and we haven't even begun to search the storeroom and the basement and the attic and under the stairs. But we have begun, and this is a very, very good start.

And now, we begin again ...

Are you willing to accept that everything single one of these fears is a story? Y or N. They are not real. They are products of your imagination. You have made them up. Sure, any of them *might* happen ... are you willing to waste your precious life on them? IF they happen at all. So what then? What if they were only ever an 'if'? Will you give your entire life to worrying about something that never, ever, ever happened? In the cold light of dawn is that sane? Y or N. Remember the spirit of the Delphic temple: know yourself. Y or N. Tell the truth.

These are questions. They are questions, no right no wrong, yours for the answering. Write your responses. Here are your relationships to your interior stories. With pen and paper, explore your relationships to your fears.

Perhaps some of the fears on your list have already happened to you. Or perhaps they've happened to someone you know. Can you separate what did happen from what *is* in your life right now? Not saying it's easy. Asking, are you willing?

Are you willing to separate your imaginary story fears from that which has already happened to you or someone you know or even someone you don't know?

Are you willing to conserve your health, so you have the capacity required to meet the challenges and crises that will rise before you in your life? For they will come. No life is exempt from them. The wheel turns.

Yes. Or no.

A long, long time ago I was a young mother living alone with small children in a lovely old house in a big city. The key to the back door was one of five you could buy over the counter from the local hardware store. Night after night I would lie in bed listening to the creaks and growls of the old house cooling with the night. I'd toss and turn seeking sleep, whilst keeping an ear out for the murderer I was sure would come this night. Front door, back door, windows, my head a riot of all the ways he would enter my home. An unwelcome shadow in the night house.

I became fed up with my story and instead of quivering in fear put my restless time to work. I began imagining what I would do when he came and created as many scenarios as there were possibilities in my head for all the ways I would defend myself and my children. I would be prepared.

Eventually I'd had enough of the whole story. Nothing ever happened. I was making myself crazy waiting for something that never, ever happened. At night I used to watch television once the children were asleep. Every night, every single night I watched a parade of women being assaulted, raped, murdered, abused, powerless at the mercy of men in the dark. So I switched it off. And I have never turned it back on. Not for stories of violence against women that had no other purpose than violence against women. They are stories. They are not benign. I switched off the fantasies of others and instantly my world became a safe place. I took my children to our local park in the dark. We walked the neighbourhood beneath the swelling moon. I brought my senses to life and I learned my world is a safe place. And if the next moment it isn't, well I would deal with that in the moment. Until then, we would live well and we would live strong and we would live free from the crippling story fears that immobilise potential for an otherwise wonderful life.

This isn't to suggest violence against women is not a phenomenally heartbreaking actuality. It is to say there is a big, big difference between 'what if' and 'what is'. Random violence is rare, and statistically, as a woman who did not live with a husband, I had a better chance of winning the lottery than being murdered.

What is your fear story?

Take each and every one of your fears, down the list, follow its thread and weave its story. Follow Ariadne's thread to the beast at the labyrinth centre. Use the question 'why?'

Why this? Is it true?

And know every time you have finished, your story begins again.

Why? Why do I fear that? Why? What will happen then? And then? And then?

Into the labyrinth. Deeper, deeper into the centre we go. Onwards, bravely onwards on your quest for the centre of your beating heart, there to confront the daemon within. Will you be devoured by the faery-beast at the centre or will you slay it, the treasure at its back yours for the claiming … only to ultimately recognise the beast was, all along, protecting your treasure.

Telling the truth as it lives in your feeling body …

Not what is right. Not what is good. Not what is safe. Much, much more than what is honest. Drill down until every cell in your body can sing *I have told the truth.*

And know this: you will never live fear-free. Story-fears are integral to human lives. You can, however, live fearlessly. Living fearlessly is not living free from fear – it is living with those fears, face on, held at bay in their proper place. *Praise the minotaur within.*

Veil 5: What do I treasure?
Things are not as they seem

I love this question. I love this question for its paradox. At first most people will say 'my children' and 'my home' and 'my partner' and 'kindness', the obvious and the surface. Or if you are isolated and disconnected from life you might say 'not much'.

Get your pen and paper and have a serious look at your treasured priorities. The purpose of the questions below is to shine a light on the tensions in your life, the push-me-pull-you demands of modern living in a competitive world. They are designed to challenge your illusions and clarify your values, root out your shames, of course, so you might truly accept yourself, as you are, and turn your attentions wholly to that which you value most thus liberating your energies to give your all to the competing desires in your life.

What do you treasure?
    Make a list.
    Now, buckle in.
    What price do you pay for that treasure? One by one. What price do you pay? Do you pay that price willingly? Or does what you claim to treasure pay a price for your illusion?

Example 1 …
    You treasure your health.
    Really? Is that true?
    Do you prioritise your health?
    Dive deeply.

What is your definition of health and what is required from you to sustain it?

Do you show up for your health? Wholly and fully and in every way your body and psyche ask from you?

Yes or no? *No right no wrong, just getting the lay of the land.*

Hard question: how is shame a part of your 'I treasure my health' story?

What are the demands on your ability to maintain your health?

Perhaps it is the need to work to sustain a particular lifestyle?

Perhaps it is your children?

Perhaps it is the absence of motivation to walk out the door again after a long day's work?

So let's ask again – what do you treasure?

Are you breaking your health to sustain the lifestyle you treasure? So what do you really treasure? Broken health or an imagined 'perfect lifestyle'?

Are you exhausted by the demands of children? So what do you really treasure? Your health or the excuse of demanding children? *No right no wrong.*

Are you breaking your health because you simply cannot make the time to meditate or go to the gym or do what you love or give up working as long as you do?

So what do you really treasure? The 'no time' story or your health?

Example 2 ...

You treasure your children. They are more important than anything else?

Really? Is that true?

Are the children you treasure out of your care for almost all of their lives?

What shame do you feel here?

What do you really treasure? Your children or your career?

Are the children you treasure staring at screens for want of a parent also staring at her screen?

What shame do you feel here?

What do you really treasure? Your children or Netflix? Your children or Instagram? *No right or wrong. No judgement.*

What do you really treasure? Your children or their exclusive schools? Your children or their ability to showcase your values?

Your children or money for your retirement?

Your children or peace and quiet while they lose themselves in a screen? Your children or your status as a perfect mother?

What do your children represent to you? Who do you need them to be? What shames do you need them to protect you from?

What shames can you not bear your children to see?

Explore your reactions to the questions. What voices explode in your head? What physical reactions land in your body? Do you split hairs with justifications and excuses? Can you allow the questions? Do you remain neutral as you read and respond to them? If you are reacting, look closer. Every reaction is our teacher. Look closer, there will be hard truth inside that reaction for you.

Remember you're in The Spiral. There are no judgements here. These are questions. Starting places. Examples of how modern stories go. Ideas worth exploring. Yours for the answering.

Example 3 …

You say you treasure kindness?

Is kindness something you offer everyone or only to those you deem worthy?

Are you kind to those you perceive see your shame? What shame do you think they see? What shame *do* they see?

Are you kind anyway?

Or are you kind only to those who make you feel safe? Who prop up your version of yourself? Who accept your mask as the woman you are?

Kindness is predicated on taking your time – are you slow and rhythmic as you go about your day or are you perpetually in a rush?

Kindness is predicated on your willingness to have conversations that are challenging for you – do you show up for outstanding conversations in your world?

If you are rushing how many small and momentary acts of kindness did you squeeze in today?

Were they obligatory responses demanded by common courtesy or kindness?

See how this goes?

What do you treasure?

Your treasure is where you put your energy. Your treasure is the effort it takes to hide your shame and the priorities in your life. Of course you must eat. Of course your children must be educated. Of course of course of course and then … then there are the illusions. And the shames. And the masks we wear. And the stories we tell ourselves so we can keep our heads above water.

What's below the surface?

You're in the swamp. Remember that. For the moment you are in the swamp. The swamp is a safe place to be. Confronting perhaps. Downright antagonising maybe. Outrageously threatening even. But it's safe. You are safe in the swamp. It's your swamp, after all. It's yours. The murk and mud, yours. The monsters in the deep, all yours. The light lines shooting through the surface above, yours too. Your one big beautiful life giving swamp.

And if the swamp threatens to overwhelm you, then reach out to a clear-eyed trusted friend of steady heart or a professional to walk with you as you navigate this journey.

So what do you treasure, really. What do you treasure?

Gently now, tell the passing truth as you know it this moment.

What do you imagine you treasure?

And what do you really treasure?

What would you love to treasure if only you were brave enough to surrender (…status…constructed self-identity…fear of having no money…exotic holidays…addiction *broad definition*…and so on)?

What do you treasure? What price are you willing to pay for what you treasure? Are you willing to do what it takes to live a treasured life you love? Answer truthfully. No right, no wrong. There is only what is. Shining the light, that's all. Aligning our values to our living. That's all.

Telling the truth as it lives in your feeling body …
Not what is right. Not what is good. Not what is safe. Much, much more than what is honest. Drill down until every cell in your body can sing *I have told the truth.*

Veil 4: What do I cling to?
My imaginary saviour

What do you tell yourself will save you?

Money? God? Your inheritance? Your children? Your partner? Being good? Being nice? Being lovely? Being sorry? Being small? Denying yourself?

More than fear, what we cling to speaks of terror.

Notebook and pen ready, feel into your body. Bring to mind what you cling to, your life raft, that which you are terrified of living without …

Are you breathless? Do tears threaten to prick at your eyes? Is your throat tight? Do you feel sick to your stomach? Are you frozen in time? Are you about to disintegrate and vanish from the Earth? If so, well, this is how you know you are on the right track.

What do you cling to? Write it out. Your life raft story, write it out. Imagine your world without your life raft and write that out too. Imagine the worst happens and write that out too.

Shame is a big part of this story. Your clinging will have everything to do with what 'they' will say. What will they say? How will this shame you *because you know they are right*? Are they right? Do you know this? How do you know this?

Take up residence for a while where your body is threatening meltdown – feel it. Breathe it. Feel it. Live it. Feel it. Release the physical hold this clinging has on you. This is how you forgo your need for the life raft. Release the physical. Write the physical release. Release and write. Release and write. It's all in the physical. It's in your body. Breathe. Breathe deeply. Surrender the physical hold this story has on you. Release and write.

Who are you without the clinging? Write your reality without the clinging. Set yourself free. Write your new story. Set others free. Stand tall and true. Look, no hands! And know. You are in The Spiral so you *know*. Life is on your side. You *know* you have everything you need to meet the challenges ahead. All that's left to you is to trust yourself. Relinquish your grip on your story about what will save you. It won't. It can't. The tides of life ensure that what we have today will be gone tomorrow. Which tomorrow we cannot know, but tomorrow you can be sure the tide will come. In the meantime we live, true to our born nature and our inherent strength and our growing courage, we live. And we trust. We trust that when we need it, our life raft will float by to save us. Until then … loosen your grip, surrender your shame and get on with your living.

Telling the truth as it lives in your feeling body …
Not what is right. Not what is good. Not what is safe. Much, much more than what is honest. Drill down until every cell in your body can sing *I have told the truth.*

Veil 3: What are my alibis?
Standing true

What do you most long to do in your life that you cannot do … because …?

What excuses do you use, often and regularly?
You know what they are.
List them.
What justifications do you store for yourself and others about why

you cannot (do any number of things you might do in a day but cannot because …)?

Start a few sentences with 'I cannot do … because …'. Fill in the blanks.

Are your alibis truthful?

Really?

Feel into your body. Tell your body your alibi. Does your body light up with joy with the liberation your alibi brings or does it contract … even in the smallest of ways at the slightest of untruths in your story?

How often do you call on your justifications and excuses?

Run through them, one by one. Where do they live in your body?

Entertain the possibility of forgoing your justifications and excuses about why you can't … and imagine stepping forward with 'yes I can'? Or 'that doesn't work for me at this time, perhaps I could suggest …'.

Are you willing to forgo your excuses and justifications? Which is another way of asking are you willing to take full responsibility for your life, right now? Or another way of asking are you willing to stop telling lies to get your own way? *No right no wrong. Just asking.*

(Oooo, did you react to the word 'lie'? If so, take a detour off the path and explore your responses. Did it feel like an accusation? An overstatement? An assault on your integrity? Has it clouded your ability to focus on the tasks at hand? Hijacked your attention? Write. Write it out. Clear the field. Find your passing truth as best you know it this moment and make your peace.)

Let's just say you said 'yes'. Yes you are willing to stop telling lies to get your own way. You will never ever again use this justification or excuse. You will either speak straight or you will do what is asked from you, head high. No excuses. No justifications. No lies. No alibi for why you 'can't'. How does this feel in your body? Close your eyes. Let the possibility rattle its way through your nervous system. Stand in the full light of day, breast to the sun, and feel your shame burn away. Pffft, just like that, mist to the shimmering light.

How much more is required from you without your alibis?
What responsibilities do you have to take?
If you accept that responsibility how is your life changed?
What new benefits come with stepping forward?
What new challenges can you foresee ahead? How will you meet them?

Remember, every small step you take forward forges new strength and new courage in you. By the time you meet the challenges ahead will be not be the same person who used alibis as excuses or justifications or as a crutch for absenting herself from responsibility.

What new challenges do you fear ahead?
Are they real? Or are they figments of your imagination?
How excited are you by the possibilities ahead in taking full responsibility for your life?
Serious question. *You're on a deep dive. Think about that.*

For the rest of your born days, watch for your excuses and justifications. Eliminate them. Stand for your truth. Stand for yourself. Stand for your life. Stand for the decisions you make, unapologetically and free from shame. Others will have something to say about it. About everything. Your life's work is not to please others. I promise you, that is not why you were born. It is to live according to your born nature on the path that unfolds before you in communion with the world into which you were born and the people among whom you live. Step forward and you will shift the power balances in your relationships. Watch for the tactics others employ to shame and limit you and mitigate your newfound strength. They may be threatened by the tide of your rising soul. That's okay. That's theirs to navigate. You may or may not be willing to offer them support, but know you cannot save them.

You probably need to know this, too: stepping out on the 'no alibis' limb can be hideously lonely at times. Others will genuinely not understand. However for every person whom you 'disappoint' or 'enrage' or from whom you reclaim your personal power, there are myriad others for whom you lead the way.

    Lead on, dear one, lead on.

Tell the truth. Not what is right. Not what is good. Not what is safe. Much, much more than what is honest. Drill down until every cell in your body can sing *I have told the truth*.

Find an old story with a frog, the original version of that which we call fairy tales. Find an old story with a frog and plaster the frog with the face of your shame*. Let shame be the mask the frog wears and you will begin to understand the role of shame in your life. The frog-bride marriage that inevitably follows? That marriage is your union with and your love for that slimy murky part of you that you are no longer willing to hide, be embarrassed by, punish yourself for, turn away from. Your frog. Your shame. Brought to light. Loved for its imperfections. Heralded for its service. To you. Whole now, you may step forward. Exposed now, you have nothing more to hide. Free now, to live your life according to your born nature, warts n all. You and your frog-bride may go to the ball. Showing up for life, as you are.

Veil 2: What is the truth I do not speak?
The sacred, revealed

There are words in the English language that contain in their letters a kind of paradoxical opposition. Sacred, scared. Live, evil. Unclear, nuclear. Earth, heart. I adore these words.

    Sacred. Your sacred self. Your scared self. One, intimately entwined with the other.

---

* With thanks to Robert Bly for interpreting the frog/shame tale.

Find a beautiful place to be. A garden. A park. A river. Somewhere wild. Somewhere more vast than you. A place to be. A mountain. The ocean. A small fire at night. A fire indoors, even if it's just a candle or two or five or fifteen. Have sustenance with you, morsels you adore, something special to drink, and for you that may be fresh clear water.

Notebook, pens. Find your place. Make yourself comfortable, close your eyes and take your time calling in *The Writer's Breath*. All the time in the world.

And now to meet that which you do not speak, not even to yourself.

What will you never ever ever speak?

That is the only question this day, this night.

What will you never speak?

It might be your longing. It might be your shame. It might be your rage. It might be your grief. What you are seeking is beyond … far beyond …

You are in new territory now. The pathways are unmapped. No one has ever been before.

What will you never speak?

Write it down. Write it out. Write tenderly. Write robustly. Find your way like a mountain climber picking a path over sliding ground. Find your footing. Find your next step. Let the mountain lead you. Let your feet lead you. Let your writing heart lead you.

What will you never speak?

You reach the top of the mountain, there to find the peak surrounded in mist. The mist is a veil. You step towards it. You are behind the veil. There to find another veil. You are dancing the mystery. Further and further you go, writing your way through the mystery of the veils. You become tangled. You keep writing. You lose your way. You keep writing. You are terrified of being lost forever. Keep writing. Keep writing. Keep going. Keep writing.

Write your way, until you punch through the veils of mist into clear blue sky.

What will you never speak?

Say it out loud.

Speak it to the mountain. Speak it to the river. Speak it to the wildflowers. Speak it to the crashing waves. Speak it to the fire. Speak it.

There is no shame here. No exile. Love, where there was no forgiveness.

Speak it soft and speak it true.

You, no longer hiding.

Welcome. It is time to turn for home.

Veil 1: What is my truth and how will I live from here?
You *do* know

What is my true purpose? It is a catchcry of our times. It drives me nuts. The insanity of people tying themselves in knots over their inability to find 'the right path', 'my true purpose', 'my life destiny' and myriad other versions of 'I was born for so much more than this'. Actually, you weren't. And, you do. You do know. You know exactly what you need to be doing. The reality is you're not brave enough to do it. What is your true path? The one you turn away from. The one for which you will not risk your money, your security, your identity … fill in the gaps with your fears about what you stand to lose.

You do know.

You know exactly what you need to be doing.

Here's how you know. There are no 'decisions' at important crossroads in our life. There is only what you know you need to do – and talking your way out of it. That's it.

So the question isn't 'what is my true purpose?' The question is 'do I have the courage to step into the unknown?' Do I have the courage to follow that faint and faraway call to 'do this', with no assurances that things will work out, with no promises that my life will be 'better'? Better than what? The agony of indecision? Do I have the courage to follow the summons within with no guarantees that I will live to see what was on the other side? Do I have the courage? Yes or no. That's it. If the answer is 'no', then make peace with your no.

That's all there is to it. Stay where you are. Forgo the endless restlessness of indecision. Raise the flag of conciliation and be content with life as you know it. And that is a perfectly fine thing to do. No right. No wrong. No judgement. Decide. That's all. Decide. Commit. Give it everything you have.

If the answer is 'yes!', then know this: you will never know where you are going. The destination is a mystery. Step forward wholly into each next step and then and only then will the step after that be revealed. This is what it is to live the mystery. There are no promises. No assurances. No guarantees. No outcomes. No reasons. No 'I deserves'. No 'I'm entitled tos'. No 'how dare yous'. No 'you owe mes'. No 'yes but what abouts'. Nope.

There is only the wild wild wonder of life, rewards that you didn't see coming and gifts you couldn't possibly have imagined, collisions that are sudden and sometimes brutal and always tumultuous until we learn to hold our centre inside the turbulence and in this way develop varying degrees of mastery until our own arrogance or pride or shame skittles us (again) and we fall flat on our faces, and from there pick ourselves up (again) and we keep going, over and over and over again. Life, on the spiral path.

So, your truth. What is your truth? *Do you hear the whisper within… there is no truth … there is only what resonates in the living body.* So how do you step forward from here? The yes path? The no path? Decide. Either way take one step at a time.

Write your way home.

And now the paradox: there is no such thing as truth. With truth comes death. You know this now. For every truth you have told throughout this writing journey there have been a thousand deaths, thus rendering the truth as you have told it no longer true. There is no truth that does not bring death. The death of shame. The death of exile. The death of petty hatreds. The death of small stories with big impacts. The death of misaligned relationships. The death of illusions. And beyond death, love. Intertwined and inseparable. Death and love. The cycle of renewal. The world remade. Love of self. Love of life. Love and compassion for others, everyone in the same boat as me. Truth and death and love. Choose one, you get all three, every time.

There is another, perhaps no less esoteric reason, for why there is no such thing as truth. When we apply words to a moment we diminish, contain and limit that which by its nature can only be experienced, and is therefore impossible to express. My Truth. Which, once reduced to words, is and was and will be forever more only a story. Isn't that disappointing? It's why we love the great poets. For they come so close.

As for the rest of us, we forgive ourselves our inability to express ourselves wholly. And we forgive others their clumsy expressions and the impossibilities of explaining themselves to us in terms we find 'acceptable'. For is that not a particular form of cruelty? The requirement that other people show up for us inside the narrow band of language and behaviour *we* require to keep our head above water? Perhaps another definition of insanity might be this: the demand that eight billion other people frame their world according to my righteous and hideously small know-nothing reality.

There is no such thing as truth. There is only law. The mystics have known it for millennia. Quantum scientists and astrophysicists, enthralled by the inimitable wonder, are bringing home the wonder through sonics and imagery. There is Law. Ours to know. And Mystery. Ours to journey, and ultimately surrender.

13-2 DEATH

MY FRIEND HAS torn up the house. I have offended his righteous sense of place in his private universe. In truth I said nothing to him that had not been said before, yet this time with two words I tripped a hair trigger of emotional chaos I had no idea rumbled beneath the surface of his world.

Pinned beneath the avalanche of his rage, I watched as my friend rampaged through the house of a writing project we shared, smashing carefully constructed ideas, taking inspired expressions of our spirits down with him. My friend failed to notice I was jammed tight beneath the boulders of his fury as he hurled our creative gifts at my feet and reduced them to matchsticks and dust.

Then he turned on me.

My friend vanished into my past and returned with trophies of my work that did not meet today's expectations and were not his to demolish. He threw those at my feet too, to mingle with the matchsticks and dust. And when the dust settled and I lay bruised and still, he offered me an explanation that smelled more like justification with no hint of apology, and I realised my friend had no idea what he had done. Frozen, I watched the quiet one inside me survey the matchsticks and dust, and there found I had nothing to say to my friend.

We had tried talking through the avalanche as he goaded me to a fight I failed to deliver, for it was not my fight. He heard nought but his own voice above the roar of his destruction. So I swallowed my words and silenced my tongue and let the landslide talk over me.

I hear myself in his wicked tongue.

In my defence, which is no defence at all before those whom I once lashed with my own wrongful insight, clever words and caustic rage, in my defence I never took aim at the creative expressions and living vulnerabilities of others when imagined slights ballooned into self-righteous fury. Like I say, no defence at all.

Bruised and silenced I survey the matchsticks and dust. I am empty. There is nothing to salvage, though of course the house I will build anew. But not here. I love my friend. I love him now in the same way I loved him before he destroyed the house. Yet I know I will not build so freely with him again, now that our future is limited to safe pathways or no pathways at all, given neither of us is likely to go out of our way to meet again. Rather than running wild through the breathtaking forest of limitless expression, my friend murdered what he imagined as threat to his existence.

There was a time I was an innocent, returning again and again and again with hope and joyful spirit to worlds destroyed. This I need do no longer. Once in this story is enough. For it was my innocence that was ambushed when my friend tore up the house. Like Snow White at the window reaching for the poisoned apple. I was foolish. I was undefended. My friend, the undisciplined warrior defending what was never under attack, lacking the awareness to short circuit things himself, had enlisted me in his story. Seamlessly I stepped in to fill the role.

As did my friend for me, for there was no way on Earth he could have torn up my house had I not invited him right on in. I had mistrusted my own creative gifts and unconsciously recruited him as their herald and their guardian protector. And there we have it, the tale of my once-friend, the sound of one heart breaking.

But that is only half the tale.

The sound of one heart breaking. Unable to bear beauty in any form, the breaking heart turns on itself. It is the unconscious human condition. Passivity, aggression, evenly matched forces of war. We are eight billion temporary life forms living on a spinning rock hurtling through space. No living human is exempt from this existence.

We are eight billion breaking hearts, at war with our own pain. In vulnerability is our strength.

The trick is learning to live *with* the breaking heart.

Death. Change. Transformation. The twist in the spiral. New beginnings. This chapter is short for no better reason than *Write Your Way Home* is in its entirety a book about death. About surrendering that which is not yours to control. About dying so something new can be born. Not a chapter preceding this one has not shone a light on that which much die so you can live. Life must be renewed. It is the law. Renewal always follows death. Law.

That masterful philosopher Alan Watts said something like this: 'When we get to thinking of everything in terms of survival and profit, then scratches on the floor cease to have magic.' Watts was referring to the wonder of children (life, renewing itself). He was referring to jaded adulthood (unsustainable on a living planet that demands renewal). He was referring to nature, and the indescribable destruction we have wreaked through immeasurable greed in the name of survival and profit. At best we might claim wilful ignorance. If you have come this far on your writing journey home that pretext is no longer available to you. For if your eyes are not open to the pretence now, then when?

Responsibility for all that you are and all that you claim to seek, when? Forgoing illusions that herald wanting and fear, when? Focussing your precious life energy on what matters most to you … when? Exactly when?

For how long do you send other people's children into the fields as fair trade for your chocolate? For how long do you imprison human beings desperate for new life on 'my' shores? *It's a planet. It's not yours.* For how long do you justify working conditions that are illegal in your own country so you might have more cheap clothes than a woman can throw away in a lifetime? These deaths are often literal. These deaths are in our ledger. The money men who profit from our greed know we will turn our well-hinged blind eye away, for as well we know by now on this journey we can justify anything. Read these statements again. They are literal. They are also metaphorical if you are willing to do a little scratching on the surface of the mirror. Grab your pen and paper. Yep, right now. Pen, paper. Writing.

Mirror, mirror, on the wall …

How do these archetypal stories, relevant and typical of our times, mirror your interior life?

What is your interior chocolate?

How do you forsake or betray the child archetype within you so you may have your chocolate and eat it too?

How do you exile yourself from your own shores?

You are imprisoned where? For how long?

What are the terms of your release?

In whose name are you punishing yourself?

Are you setting an example to others?

How do you justify your imprisonment – your 'we are saving lives' save face story lie?

How do you justify the sweat shop hours you put into a job or lifestyle you hate?

Who do you resent for this state of affairs?

Those cheap clothes you purchase only to throw away, what is their interior correlation?

As within, so without. As above, so below. It is the law.

In speaking of the dying Canadian Stephen Jenkinson says this: 'So what do dying people need from the rest of us? They need the rest of us to know something enduring and true and useful about what dying is and what it asks from us all, and they need us to be able to act on this wisdom when the time comes.' He adds: 'And that time is always coming.'

Jenkinson's reference is literal. He is referring to people who are dying. This reference may be pertinent to you in its literal sense at this point in your life. It applies equally to every interior death you/we personally endure, small and large, and small with large legacies, and large only to be revealed as small. Death is our ally. Death is our opportunity to start afresh. Death says you, now. And you, but not yet. Death demands our attention. And it demands we show up. And, if we are to show up, best we know something enduring and true and useful about what dying is.

And that requires us to be able to read the word, feel the word, speak the word: Death. The 13th card in the major arcana. The twist in The Spiral. Death. Metaphorical. Literal. Death. Change. Death. Love. Death. Truth. Death. Reckoning. With or without your consent. Death, on every breath you take.

> *Because I could not stop for Death,*
> *he kindly stopped for me.*
>
> Emily Dickinson

The Sacred, Said
The final reckoning

Pen, paper. Feet on the floor. *The Writer's Breath.*

Death is a positive force

Is this statement challenging for you?

If yes, why?

Explore your responses to this short sentence: Death is a positive force.

Describe how it feels in your body.

Do you want to shut it down? Run away? Argue the point?

Do you want to annihilate the stupid person who said it?

We are speaking of one sentence. Five words. Death is a positive force. What is your response to these five words?

If this statement is not challenging for you, why not?

What is your story about death as a positive force? Show up.

You have written not a modicum of truth to this answer until you are uncomfortable, unsure of your certainty that death is a positive force.

Not because you have to change your mind but rather, to examine the probability that arrogance or pride or … (your personal transgressor) may be preventing you from deeper exploration.

Death belongs in the realm of Mystery.

No one short of mastery is comfortable with Mystery.

Death is a positive force …

What situations in your life would you willingly transform in a blink?

Write them out. Give them all the blah you've got.

What in your life would you willingly transform now?

What are you waiting for? Write!

What are you waiting for?

Why haven't you acted before now?

Why not now?

What are you waiting for?

What impossibility has to be perfect before you take the action you already know you have to take?

What must die if you act?

What promises of safe passage do you require?

Death is a positive force …

Are you willing to risk the possibility there is no such thing as failure?

Are you willing to shift your measure of success?

Can you define success as a willingness to act, regardless of assurances of outcomes?

Can you eliminate the idea of success all together? There is, after all, no failure if there is no possibility of success.

The wheel turns. The spiral twists.
Success will always lead to failure.
Failure will always lead to success.
It is the law.

Death is a positive force …
Can you trust death?
Can you act?
What is the price to be extracted from you if you do not act?
What is the price to be paid if you do act?
Are you willing to pay the price? *Can't get it right, can't get it wrong.*
There's only what you can live with. Either way, you'll never know what the other path had in store for you.
Decide. Decide now. Commit.
To act. Or not to act. Commit.
Your focus, here and only here.
No what ifs. No buts. No shoulds. Commit.
What discipline is required from you to meet this positive force?
What discipline is required if you turn away?
Imagine you choose to die, now. Head high, you meet this positive force.
What is enduring here?
What is true?
What is useful?
And how will you put this wisdom to work on your own behalf, now, in this place?

A word on life's balance sheet …
Go on if you dare. Sift everything you do from here on through the unsubtle undercurrents of survival and profit. Gauge the impact of this balance sheet on your choices, your vote, your life, the lives of others.
And answer this: what price should others pay for your survival and profit? *No right, no wrong, just working out the balance sheet.*

Telling the truth. And letting death come. You have no choice now, you have come too far.

Develop a check list: assets, gold stocks, superannuation, private education, your second house in a holiday mecca, your fence with the locked gate, your just rewards for your 'I work hard' story and so on. *No right no wrong. No judgement.*

What price do others – people and animals – pay for your survival and profit?

What price should others pay for your living? *No right no wrong. No judgement. Life is a survival game.*

Everything you have. Including that which you don't even know you have, such as privilege. *Examine it. Examine what? It's right there in your immediate turning away.*

Power, in the naming. Shedding light on the unshamed, in the naming. Restoration to a world you actually want to live in, in the naming.

What price do others pay for your survival and profit?

What price do you pay for your survival and profit?

That change everyone seems to want these days? It starts here.

You are going to die anyway.

How will you live from here?

Are you willing to loosen any of the ties that bind you?

That bind others?

That bind you to others?

We are one, you know. One and the same.

What you do to one you do to the whole.

It is the law.

Speak your life …

What would you like people to say about you at your funeral?

Write your eulogy, about who you know yourself to be. Be real. Be honest. Unmask. Tell them the whole of the gentle best about your disappointments and your victories. Share your overcomings.

Refrain from speaking about others. Speak only for yourself. Only of yourself. As if your best self is doing the speaking, compassionate and tender on your behalf.

Write your eulogy.

Speaking your life ...

What do you fear people would say about you at your funeral?

Write this eulogy. Put words into specific people's mouths.

Are you willing to let these imaginary voices die?

Can you bury your shame so you might live?

Are you willing to return from exile, self imposed and otherwise?

Are you willing to forgo your need to exile others, so you might be 'safe'?

Can you step forward for yourself, forgive yourself that which has been so merciless in the interior life?

Hold a funeral for this imaginary self. Put her on the pyre of her living grief and consequential follies, and send her up in flames.

Now, light a new fire beneath another starry sky and revisit your eulogy. Put your best self forward and refine that which you wrote in the first version. Landmark your wonder. Celebrate your living. Put yourself at the centre of creation. Because that is where you belong.

Here we meet the inherent wonder of the breaking heart. Your heart. Your living breaking heart. Write her story. Sing it out. Sing it true. The true story of your heart. Wounded and whole. Tender and true. Broken and breaking and strong.

Whether death/change comes for you or you make a move towards death/truth, there is nothing reasonable about change. You cannot reason your way out of change. You cannot reason your way through it. You are beyond the realm of reason. And this is why death breaks us apart. There is nothing you can do. There is nothing you could do. Change is out of your hands. Your task is to ride out the storm. For inside your broken heart is your living. Here is your vulnerability.

Here is your compassion. Here is your forsaking of self above others and inside that your peace with life, on Earth. Nothing to defend. No wars to fight. Your doubts revealed. Your shames, withering in the light. Here you stand, visible, exposed, your wounds evident, your breaking heart proof of your passing this way. You have lived and you have survived and you are witnessed. Mainly, you have done your duty in passing on tips to the travellers who have yet to pass this way.

Write her story. Write her story. Write her story.

And raise a glass to the same rising moon that sang to the entirety of the human ones who came before you.

Thank you. Mothers fathers all. Thank you.

We all long to be witnessed.

In death comes the witnessing.

Here is everything you long for.

Everything.

Death, so all might live.

Death, so all might love.

13-3 LOVE

MANY, MANY years ago I was completely at a loss as to what to do with my life. The winds of circumstance had blown me east to a distant land, spun me around and blown me right back home again. Once landed, I had no what to do. No idea where to be. So I bought a car. I drove the coast. I slept in the back of the wagon, spending my days reading and walking the beaches. I was utterly lost, living a beachnik's paradise.

I got down to my last fifty dollars. Fifty dollars between me and starvation, proverbial and literal. I sat on the wide green headland that was my point of return each night, the light of brightest blue above and the deep of ocean blue below, and stared at the $50 note. I decided I would have a yoga lesson, a private session with my former teacher. I found her number. I rang her from the phone box outside a shop near the headland (it was the 90s). I booked my lesson for 6am the next day.

The following morning I woke in darkness and drove south to my lesson. I was early, so I drove on to nearby Broken Head. As I stood on the dunes looking out at the eastern horizon, the morning crisp and clean, I marvelled that in all the years I'd been driving this coastline I had never previously stopped at Broken Head. I ran down the golden dune towards the water, the sand cold on my bare feet. And I walked along the water's edge as the rising sun lit the morning gold. The waves, small and gentle, white and frilly, ran the sand to lap at my feet. Whoosh, shoosh, they broke in tiny tumbles, coming and going, coming and going.

I was lost. My spirit overwhelmed with my lack of direction

and purpose. Bathed in the beauty of the Earth, deeply connected to our natural world, I was without bearings in the realm of human endeavour, outside community and connection. As the sun popped golden above the horizon I turned my heart to the light and with all the passion and fullness of a breaking heart I raised my eyes to the light and asked the entire universe a billowing, bellowing question – 'what's it for?'

To this day, I have no idea whether I spoke that question aloud or not.

'What's it for?' Immediately I glanced down at the wet sand, just as a small wave tipped a lacy frill onto my feet before making its run for deeper waters. And there, on the damp and spotted sand, just near my toes, lay a small green heart. I stared, bent slowly to pick it up. I held the polished green heart, the size of my thumbnail, between my fingers. I held it up to the light. I stared in wonder at the precious gift – the answer to my question. Not a stone whose shape resembled a heart, but a polished green heart. Trinket or precious jewel, as others have often asked me, I neither know nor care. I have my answer and that is value enough.

What's it for?

It is for love.

This whole human journey is for love.

And so we enter the final mystery. Love. It's what the living do. It's who we are. If this life is for anything, it is for that. You are for love. I am for love. We are love. That's it. The sum total. Nothing left to say. Nothing left to do. No-one more special than any other. No-one more deserving of your love. No-one more or less deserving of anyone else's love. It's just love. The whole dance. Love. That is the only thing of value to living humans on this Earth. Love. Life force. *The Writer's Breath*. Let it run. You. Love. The Whole. It's the law.

And now, to our final writing journey. Questions to excavate the heart. Find your place. Notebook and pen. Feet. Earth. *The Writer's Breath*. Come home. Come in. One whole being breathing in time with an entire universe. All that is outstanding, now brought to the light. The questions are random. They are for you and about you, only you.

From the top …

What is your agenda?

We all have them. They are inside every encounter, every thought, every plan we make for life to go our way. What is your agenda? And now: is it loving? Is your agenda loving?

How differently might or will you express your agenda now it is measured by your loving?

What are you trying to prove?

To whom? Why? What for? What's the impact on your life of this endless proving? What happens if you lay this burden down? Can you? Do you want to? Can you write a new ending for the proving?

What would Love do in this place?

Where do you abandon yourself?

Why? Or don't even bother with why, cut straight to the chase – what are you going to do about it?

What does Love ask from you here?

Do you deserve acknowledgement, recognition?

For what? Says who? What do you do that is unacknowledged and unrecognised? Is it healthy for you to act this way? How else might this story go?

What story does Love tell in this place?

List your grievances. All of them.

You know what you need to do. Give them all the writing what for and then either take action or drop 'em. Be done.

What would Love do?

And now ...

Are you making right use of the gifts and talents you were blessed with in this life?

Do you withhold them, from yourself and/or others? Do you use them as a weapon? What is the right use of the gifts and talents you were born with?

What does Love ask from you?

And what about this ...

What will you not allow in others?

Ouch, I know right. What will you not put up with, choke the life out of? What causes you to pounce and shut down the happy expressions of others? What do you despise and how does it threaten you?

Can you let Love come through the slammed door? Describe Love's entry into this place.

Deeper now ...

Are you being left behind?

Where? How? Why? What do you fear? Whose life are you living? How does Love hold you here?

Is it love? Or Love?

And now ...

Are you still hiding?

What will it take for you to come out of hiding? You know the drill, we've been through questions like this before. Cut straight to it. You tried so hard and they just don't get it. Compassion now. Write your hiding story and come out come out wherever you are.

Can you take Love's hand and come out come out wherever you are?

And this ...

What is your loneliness story?

What does nobody understand? Are you ashamed of this story?

Do you hide it? Write your loneliness story and please don't say at this late stage in the game you don't have one.

What place Love in your lonely story?

Deeply now ...

What is your soul seeking?

Simple really.

Ride the wind of Love. What is your soul seeking ...

Deeper still ...

What would your world look like if your priority was the human heart?

How would you go about your living? What is outstanding if you live from this place? Your grievances, what place do they have in a world where the human heart is your priority? Write this new story. Test it out on your living flesh. How does it feel in your body?

What would your world look like if your priority was the human heart? If your dance was the dance of Love. Only Love. What would your world look like if Love was your priority?

Home. You are home. You have ventured out from the centre of the Spiral, there to wind your way to centre once more. And here we have it, your writing journey done. Here to begin again. For sure and for certain the next twist in the spiral will come. Until then, keep writing. Stalk your living. Know that it is far more important at this stage in your journey to be aware of the feelings that land in your body than to give oxygen to the story you tell. The story is nothing. It's a story. The meaning you give people and encounters and events – pure story. Yours to tell as you please. It is your response to the story that matters, that determines your future and creates the reality you and those around you and even those you will never meet will be living. It's not the stories you tell that matter, it's your relationship to your stories. Mercy at the centre.

From here, catch entanglements and constrictions and sudden barbs before they land in your body, release them as quickly as you can if they do land. Your thoughts, your feelings, your emotion stories, your body: 'go to the pages', as my friend Mary would say. Write your way through a sudden entanglement. Here is the entirety of your responsibility: my body, my thoughts, my aches, my heaven. There is enough to do without minding other people's business as well.

Return to right use of language. Everything is not a crisis. Almost nothing is a crisis. Forgo the need to overstate *everything*: depressed, anxious, awesome, amazing, brilliant, wonderful. Take the time to find the words that express what you truly mean, how you actually *feel*.

Recognise the age of reason, like the age of matter, is over. Life is change. Change is not reason-able. Matter has given way to energy. Nothing is solid. There are vast spectra of intelligence available to all living organisms. I'll leave it to you to determine what this means for your life.

And now, welcome traveller. Welcome home. Rest. Put your feet up. Drink up. Sup well. To everything there is a season. To every spiral a twist. The turning times will come. Truth. Death. Love. You know now, in every cell in your body you know, that you have everything you need to step forward on the journey when the whisper rises within, calls you out, trills your name, again. Until then, breathe easy. Even then, breathe easy. For now you know what it's for.

It is for Love.

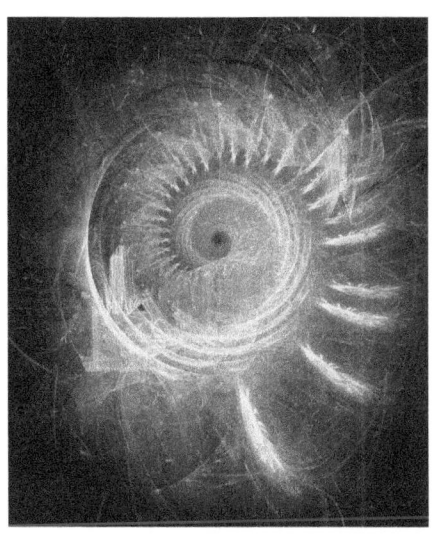

Thank you Artemis, for teaching me how to hunt.
Karen Elliott

© Stephanie Dale, 2024
International Wellbeing-through-writing Institute
www.iwwi.com.au

www.ingramcontent.com/pod-product-compliance
Lightning Source LLC
Chambersburg PA
CBHW062057290426
44110CB00022B/2617